THE FREEDOM MANIFESTO

THE FREEDOM MANIFESTO

VERNE ATRILL

Dimensionless Science Publications Limited
Suite 2202, 425 First Street SW, Calgary, Alberta,
Canada, T2P 3L8

ISBN (USA and Canada) 0-9691001-0-8

To John Falconer

"... government even in its best state is but a necessary
evil; in its worst state an intolerable one..."

Thomas Paine, in *Common Sense*.

EDITOR'S INTRODUCTION

The Freedom Manifesto shows how inflation can be stopped, how insolvent governments can be returned to solvency, and how both those ends can be achieved by voluntary means.

The means derive from the principles of Dr. Atrill's life-work: Objective Economics. In his introduction to the author's first book, *How* ALL *Economies Work*, Dr. Warren J. Blackman, Professor of Monetary Theory at the University of Calgary, wrote: "*The physical sciences are concerned with the observation of nature and in the discovery of natural laws which govern natural phenomena. It so happens that throughout all these laws there exists one over-riding principle and that is that Nature always directs her affairs with an economy of effort, and it is precisely this economy of effort, which means the attainment of the highest possible level of efficiency, that the businessman shares with Nature in his attempts to remain solvent...*

"*The physicist in the process of arriving at Nature's laws has discovered some mathematical constants which define some important relationships, among these being the speed of light. Incredible as it might seem these same constants are observed in Objective Economics and it is to the credit of Verne Atrill's mathematical genius that he has derived them quite independently of the physical sciences...*

"*Does this mean that men in pursuit of their economic objectives are governed by the same natural laws that exist in the science of physics? The answer is yes, and will continue to be so as long as humans follow the general rule of economy of effort in their economic processes. Dimension-less physics and Objective Economics are in truth sister sciences and the early efforts of the Physiocrats to discover the natural laws governing the economic system of their day are justified . . ."*

In *The Freedom Manifesto*, Dr. Atrill has applied the principles of his Objective Economics to the daily affairs of business that affect us all. They are rooted in the balance sheet. By examining the balance sheets, extending over a seven-year period, of the 300 companies in the Composite Index of the Toronto Stock Exchange, the author has demonstrated the truth of a fundamental principle of his science. It is that the state of an entity—whether a corporation, an individual or a government—is determined by certain values of the debt structure ratio (the ratio between what is owed to, and owed by, the entity, i.e. between its receivables and its payables). The author explains how rising and falling values of that ratio reflect the entity's solvency.

The single entity which can prolong a state of insolvency is a money-issuing government. The continued presence in an economy of such an insolvency, and the pressures thereby imposed upon the solvent entities in the rest of the economy, are the primary cause of inflation. Thus central banks, which perform the money-issuing function, are the devices that maintain their governments' insolvencies.

In analyzing the whole banking function, the author shows how governments have been able to sustain deficits beyond the point at which any entity but government would be forced to declare bank-ruptcy and sell assets. By creating central banks, governments disarmed the private banks whose application of normal business practices would have halted governmental extravagance.

It is no accident, therefore, that Thomas Paine's admonition appears on the frontispiece. *The Freedom Manifesto* calls on govern-ments to get out of the business of trying to create wealth, which they are unsuited for, and to get back into the business of governing, which only they can do. It calls on citizens to exercise their freedom by passively resisting government's attempts to borrow from them. Instead, the business community, and the financial community which supports it, should devise instruments that, by offering both stability and an assured return, are more attractive than government debt. Finally, it calls on the investment community to construct an equity issue of historic proportions, an issue whose successful sub-scription would return the Government of the United States, and other governments, to solvency.

The Freedom Manifesto challenges economists, businessmen, politicians and public servants to re-examine the economics that un-derlies all business and politics. It suggests solutions that derive not from subjective theory but from demonstrated facts. In doing so, it offers the prospect of bridging the political gap that divides east and west; Stuart Chase's "tyranny of words" stands to be resolved in the language of mathematics.

Kenneth McDonald

CONTENTS

AUTHOR'S PREFACE

To write about freedom, and to borrow the word Manifesto from the title of the work by Marx and Engels that was published in 1848, is of course an intentional slight to communism. Whatever else they wrote about in their *Communist Manifesto*, it was not freedom. One hundred and thirty-three years later the practice of communism is diametrically opposed to freedom; its threat to what freedom remains continues to grow.

Obvious as those facts are to at least half the world, the main theses of this book are not obvious, although many suspect they are true. They are that in both the east and the west scholars have failed to develop a useful scientific understanding of how ALL economies work, east, west, north and south. That failure has created two slaveries, not one. One slavery is to communism. The other, and I think the more frightening, is slavery to inflation.

This second slavery is more serious for two reasons. One is the obvious fact that after more than a decade of avowed attempts to limit and diminish inflation, we must concede that we have failed. No one can project that failure much into the future without the deepest concern. The other reason is that it is in the west, i.e. the half of the world where we have been more aware of inflation the longer that we hold to the conceit that we *do* understand how economies work. So strong are we in that conceit that we have built a whole empire which is concerned exclusively with "running the economy". Starting with the ill-advised International Monetary Fund (IMF) and developing tentacles into every central government in the west through other supra-national bodies such as the Organization for Economic Cooperation and Development (OECD), the World Bank, the organization of central banks, central banks themselves and so on, "running economies" has become one of the largest businesses in the west.

Plainly, that empire has failed to control inflation. That the empire itself has been a basic cause of inflation is not so plain. In fact, we must dig very deeply into how economies work before we can understand how it has been possible to defraud the taxpayer so long and so extensively with the illusion that the empire is necessary, that it performs vital functions, and that its existence does not create the very problems it sets out to cure. Once we recognize that illusion, we can see how fundamental it has been to the empire's growth that large and influential sections of society be picked up in its tweedledum and tweedledee debates of Monetarism vs Keynesianism, Keynesianism vs Neo-Keynesianism, monetary targetting and interest float vs interest rate targetting and monetary float. These are the semantics of an "economese" whose acceptance prevents us from recognizing the fraud perpetrated on us while allowing us to share in the great illusion that we know what we are talking about. They are the pomp and circumstance without which the profession of economics would not exist in its present form.

Damning economic doctrines, however necessary that may be, is not what this book is about. Rather does it advance a positive approach to the world economy, to national economies, and particularly to our own private economic activities that will be effective in halting inflation. The most immediate prize held out by the title of the book, therefore, is freedom from at least one of our two slaveries. In grasping that freedom, it is argued that the slavery to communism, the other slavery, will be weakened.

The main positive doctrine advanced in the book is that we must passively resist the insolvent central governments which these empires of economese have created and whose insolvency is the sole cause of inflation. In doing that we must school ourselves against creating a new empire to replace the one we will inevitably destroy. The world needs no new empires and it has several too many now. What we must do is learn again to mind our own business and make sure that others, in minding theirs, do not hurt ours. Our best defence against that is not another rash of laws and another empire of pseudo-intellectuals imposing their dialectic upon us as they create and coerce us into maintaining even more insolvencies. It is a vigorous return to the disciplines of a banking system freed from subversion by central banks whose sole business is to keep their insolvent clients, central governments, feeding at the economy's troughs.

When I say that, however, I am in no sense advocating a "pig philosophy", to use Carlyle's expression, as our dominant economic idea. Kindness, charity, open-handedness are in no way prohibited by freely operating economies. As the British economist, Senior, emphasized, what we *do* with our prosperity is also our own business. We have no reason to think that we will hurt our fellow man with it more than we will help him.

If we can bring inflation under control, break our slavery to it, by passively resisting every move of our governments to sustain their insolvency, then the only economic idea I wish to convey is one of humility in face of the domain of natural law in which we discover the economy to be. We have every reason to be both humble and frightened as the power of that domain of activity is revealed to us by the principles of Objective Economics, the major discoveries underlying this book. That spirit of humility and fear will return us to the point in history at which the organized study of economy began. No truthful reading of any of the great classical authors, Dr. François Quesnay, Dr. Adam Smith, Reverend Thomas Malthus, or David Ricardo, reveals anything but that they sought *natural* laws of what they felt was a domain of *nature*, namely, the economy. Each of those authors in his own way, was trying to "pull off a Newton." Objective Economics finally discovers some of the principles they sought.

It is because the present thesis and Objective Economics owe so much to these authors and subsequent authors such as Alfred Marshall who were much influenced by their writings, that we can claim only a new synthesis of the literature. The many new tools the new science gives us create the illusion of a new economics but such is not the case. Although its standard bearers often tripped and nearly fell, the banner of economics as a *natural* science rather than a subjective discipline continued to be held aloft throughout the dark period in our literature which began with J.S. Mill's *Principles of Political Economy* (1848), and brought us through more than 125 years of subjective economics to culminate in the irrelevancy of modern macroeconomics.

Alfred Marshall and Friedrich Hayek have been perhaps more important than most as standard bearers of an economics of natural law. Both have had special care and preoccupation with the "time problem" which neither would accept had been resolved by the subjective economics. I think also that both have had or would have had (in Marshall's case) great difficulty in accepting the "mathematicizing" of economics that has followed from developments in mathematics in the latter half of the 19th century. In large part those developments must be seen as freeing mathematics, particularly the calculus, from its original ties to physics. In no sense do they follow from economics discovering its own mathematics. If we speak in rigor, it was only after that freedom was achieved, *if* it truly was, that economics had any right to the calculus and other extremum analytical tools.

This is why Jevons, writing in 1871, the year prior to the landmark papers of Weierstrass and Dedekind, seemed to find his "mathematics" an encumbrance; Marshall, writing in 1890, found his mathematics interesting if not exciting and well worth placing in an Appendix; Fisher, writing in 1892, tried to achieve a synthesis with his mathematics in a major mathematical work; and Samuelson, writing in 1948, did achieve a running synthesis of literal and mathematical thought applied to economics. The intellectual process inherent to this chain of events was a growing realization that once the calculus was cut adrift from the physical concepts of space and time, i.e. of "at rest" and "in motion" and based upon number alone, then the mathematics of economics, namely constrained optimalization, had already been written by Lagrange and Euler and a few others by the end of the 18th century. Of all economic authors, N. Georgescu-Roegen offers the most detailed statement of this debt and problems that have arisen from it in his *The Entropy Law and the Economic Process*. See in particular his Chapter III and Appendix A.

It is interesting that both the British school with Marshall and the Austrian with Hayek had standard bearers of natural economic law within them. That I missed studying under Hayek at the London School of Economics by one year was a great disappointment to me but it was more than compensated by the challenge of study under Lionel Robbins, the world's foremost standard bearer of the subjective economics. It is a signal tragedy that the doctrine of subjectivism he represents, and that returned economic studies to an Aristotelian means-ends teleology, has enslaved the world by its failure to identify itself, i.e. its practice, as the fundamental cause of inflation.

Scientific error has surprising ways of forcing itself on the public mind. The Reagan Administration in the United States is currently serving as its instrument. Rarely can there have been an election in which professional doctrines were so much at issue so publicly. Friedman took most of what his Monetarism has to say into a public television series called "Free to Choose", a popularization I suspect no scholar could watch comfortably. A new expression has been coined, "Supply-Side Economics", that I suspect no scholar can hear or use without blushing and that must disturb the eternal rest of Ricardo and Marshall at least. The manipulators of the alleged control mechanisms in the economy such as the Federal Reserve System, rather than admitting that they neither understand nor can control what is happening, allow whole sections of the population to damn them for their hard hearts. It is upon this triumvirate of alleged knowledge that an apparently decent man, President Reagan, has decided to rest his case and his place in history.

I believe the whole structure will fail of its avowed purpose of controlling and diminishing inflation. This will happen because at no place in it is there a correct, scientifically relevant understanding of what inflation is and how insolvent governments, including that of the United States, by their very economic existence, continue to cause it. Making governments solvent is the task we all must face. The cosmetics of balancing budgets as compared with the need for massive sales of government assets simply will not suffice.

This book is dedicated to my publisher, Mr. John Falconer, of Calgary, President of Dimensionless Science Publications Limited. His patience as I tried to get it down on paper while every day taught me more of the principles of Objective Economics has been fundamental. Part of it was written at his villa on Maui in Hawaii, part was written in Toronto, part in Quebec's Laurentians, and part while 30,000 feet in the air as I crossed and recrossed much of the world. It is fitting that these final words are being written in the Laurentians for it was here more than a decade ago that I was informed that the Prime Minister of Canada, Pierre Trudeau, wanted me to go ahead with the Great Plains Project. That project brought me into communication with many of the most distinguished developmental scientists and executives in Canada and other countries. Coinciding with my finally being able to formulate mathematically problems in the literature that had begun to bother me even before I went to the London School of Economics in 1950, my vision of the economy was forced into an empirical mold at a crucial juncture by that project. It has never left that mold even as the theory of Objective Economics becomes more and more complex.

My debts to Professors Warren Blackman and David Cape are made clear in the text and many more people who are not mentioned have contributed as well. As was the case for my *How* ALL *Economies Work*, the encyclopaedic mind of Mr. Murray Stewart has remained available for my picking. Between 1979 when that book was published and now I have come to know some of the political thought of Professor H.S. Ferns of the University of Birmingham. As a result, I have recognized that I stand by no means alone with several parts of the thesis of this book.

A special word must be said about Mr. Kenneth McDonald, the editor of the book. First of all it bothers my sense of the military tradition that I learned to respect on the battlefields of Italy that he always presents himself in his writings as *Mr.* rather than *Group Captain* which is his substantive rank. Had I made it through from junior to senior officer I should not have let people forget it. Secondly, his efforts have been painstaking on my behalf. They have far exceeded the functions of editorship. I must say, however, that whatever faults remain with the book, they are my responsibility, not his.

My gratitude is owed to Mrs. Mary Sandison and Mrs. Myrtle Berger. They have mastered the art of keeping typescripts straight when I continually changed my mind about them, while retaining the high good humor conducive to work.

I have continued to try the patience of the Dutch lady who married me at the end of the Second World War, and have never found it wanting. That this book has been completed at all follows from the professional skills of doctors and nurses at Ste. Agathe des Monts in Quebec and Sunnybrook Hospital in Toronto.

June, 1981
St. Adolphe de Howard
Quebec, Canada

PART 1

THE TWO SLAVERIES

CHAPTER 1

Summary of the Argument

The world is gripped by two slaveries. One is the slavery to inflation, a circumstance that has arisen mainly in the west and is now penetrating the east. The other is the slavery to communism. Although it mainly affects the east, as an on-going regime, substantial bridgeheads exist in the west.

Both of these slaveries have resulted from disciplines of thought about how economies work. Underlying each is an "economics" which is elevated by its proponents to the status of a "science". In the perspective of this book and that of the technical book preceding it, *How* ALL *Economies Work*[1], both of these economic disciplines are in gross error.

The tragedy is that the world's scholars, split into two camps, have enslaved the world by error, technical error. That they achieved this with the best intentions only adds to the tragedy for it is far more difficult to castigate and cast out good people than it is bad ones. Indeed, goodness is very easily confused with scientific rectitude. That economic writers in both of these incorrect views of how economies work have been "on the side of the angels", have stressed human misery, and have tried conscientiously to alleviate it, is a factor of some consequence for it obscures both the nature and extent of mankind's slavery.

Claiming to be scientists, and believing their causes to be good, economists promote their disciplines with fervor. This missionary zeal marks a significant break with tradition. A quarter of a century ago and more, distinguished thinkers such as Frank H. Knight, Lionel Robbins, and many others, clearly understood that their economics, essentially the subjective economics of the west, could not be freed from a belief that events are influenced by design and purpose. As a result, their economics could not be freed from the charge that it interpreted the world process in a particular way that could not be tested. Recently N. Georgescu-Roegen in his *The Entropy Law and Economic Process*[2], has made the same point in great detail and impressive erudition. None of these authors expressed pride in that fact and all, I think, would prefer that it not be so. Today's economists, however, seem to be proud of the fact and look forward eagerly to the better world their "born again" mentality will supposedly yield to us.

They do so despite overwhelming evidence that the economics of both the west and the east lie right at the heart of the world's troubles. Economists of the west failed to develop a science of solvency that would allow them to understand, and allow governments to understand, the serious results of governments being led into the insolvency that causes inflation; those results were no less than to make government the enemy of the people. The economists (whether of the east or the west) who follow the Marx-Lenin-Mao tradition, on the other hand, have allowed their theories of struggle and of exploitation to pass untested into doctrines that are still in the vanguard of the world marketing of communism.

Neither of these traditions offers any prospect of improvement; both threaten our survival.

The initiative in the west rests not with economists, but with other professionals and lay people who are deeply concerned about a world society that will not unify, and terrors that keep on repeating themselves with broader sweeps. The sheer numbers of such people can achieve much with passive resistance to government.

And it *is* government that must be resisted even though governments are not to blame. Their condition merely reflects the failure of the economic disciplines to allow governments to understand themselves, to understand what they have been doing to the rest of society. Nevertheless it is government that must be stopped in its mad race to the insolvency that underlies our inflation. It must be stopped because it will not stop itself. People, not governments, commit suicide.

Passive resistance to insolvent governments must be our mode of action in the western world. It carries a great responsibility, for if our resistance is not passive it will push government out of the tradition of human liberty. Fortunately, closing our pocketbooks to any borrower is an act that can be carried out quietly, with dignity, and almost without detection. Just as we conferred solvency on government originally, so can we remove its insolvency.

One can be sanguine about the west. Passive resistance that liquidates governments is feasible. It can happen and happen peacefully. Proposition 13 in California is evidence that much can be done without taking to the streets. Even without such popular movements, however, refusal to buy government debt by perhaps as few as 500 large buyers per country would quickly force insolvent governments to liquidate assets and diminish their roles in the economy. Convincing those 500 to adopt such a policy is a manageable task. So is the task of convincing the investment community that new debt and equity instruments which compete with those of the government can find a home in the market.

Government depends upon the investment community—its trading connection—to market its debt issues. In time, that community has come to depend upon the activity as a major source of income. But it need not do so. That trading connection can devise private issues that compete favorably with those of government, and reduce both government's insolvency and its own contribution to it in the process.

We have not recognized the power of the trading connection of government because we have not understood that liquidity—which in its broadest sense is the ability to sell equity and debt instruments in the marketplace—cannot be legislated. This is one of the discoveries of Objective Economics[3]. Rather than being created by legislative acts and fiat—"forcing" paper instruments on the market—liquidity

is the product of the trading connections that define, and are defined
by, the economic state of any entity in the economy, including government. The valuation process through which price is arrived at is
nature's way of ensuring that the liquidity consistent with that economic state is generated, and that that state is consistent with that
liquidity. As these facts become more widely understood, so will governments' trading connections be seen as the primary target of an
appeal for passive resistance to insolvent governments. I have already found willingness to stop aiding and abetting governmental
insolvency in that target area. I repeat, we can be sanguine in our
hopes for the west.

Hope is harder to come by for the east. Perhaps the west's only
realistic objective in its eastern thrust is building the scientific
knowledge of how economies work so as to weaken the marketing
thrust of international communism. I am not, I think, naive about
the real limitations to democratic processes in the west but there is
no doubt that, however great those limitations may be, they are far
exceeded in the east. The major communist regimes are armed
camps, as difficult to get out of as to get into. Ever since Stalin was
able to take advantage of Trotsky's absence (on holiday) when Lenin
died, and build his regime unopposed[4], this iron rule has characterized communist regimes, not only in the Soviet Union but in China,
Cuba, and many satellite states of the east. It is indeed their style of
government. Whatever it means to the people, and I have the impression that in Quaker terms "it is not as bad sometimes as it is
other times", it makes passive resistance almost irrelevant because
the dependence of the regimes on cooperation is, and always has
been, minimal. Certainly, nothing like a sensitive money market
trading connection for government exists. Removing cooperation,
therefore, is meaningless.

Whatever hopes I have for the east come from a totally different
direction. They are based upon the wide network of scientific inter-
changes going on east-west, particularly in the physical and mathematical fields. Objective Economics, and especially the dimensionless
science of observation of which it is a part, will be of deep interest
particularly to scientists of the Soviet Union, because the science
heralds practical applications of discoveries largely made by Russians.
There is some specific precedent for hope in this respect because

whereas the subjective economics of the west is of no interest in the east, and is in fact not even taught, operations research and linear and non-linear programming, which have been largely developed by economists of the west, are taught, and are used. I believe the thrust of the new mathematics of dimensionless science will be even stronger.

For a number of reasons, it is possible that a deep understanding of the discoveries of Objective Economics will arise first in the east. Whatever official doctrinaire views might oppose it, there is no "economic establishment" that must step aside to let the new science penetrate. Missing, too, is the near-universal language of the macro concepts (GNP, GNE, BOP, etc.) that shouts at us in all media. Even the extension of the west's economic establishment into supranational bodies (OECD, the IMF, the World Bank, the group of central banks, etc.) is largely irrelevant to the east. If my assessment of these probabilities is correct, and the east proves receptive not only to Objective Economics but also to its potential, mentioned in note 3, for predicting the stock market, the prospect is sobering indeed. One does not relish the vision of the east being able to predict the stock markets of the west, particularly if the economic establishment of the west has been able to slow down the penetration of Objective Economics to such an extent that we in the west lack the competence to predict them. This vision is not fanciful. A generation that can walk on the moon can, given the tools of Objective Economics, predict the visible equity markets whether they are in New York, London, Tokyo, or Toronto. Such ability in the hands of an enemy would be devastating, because ability to predict is ability to control. Its application would be almost undetectable, but its repercussions across the target economies could be colossal.

My decision, in writing about freedom, to draw heavily on data taken from the real world, was deliberate. Fallacies must be dispelled by facts. The vital issue is to achieve understanding that the subjective economics which absolutely dominates both our thought and our actions in the west is wrong, wrong, wrong. Argument, of which there has been a surfeit, cannot achieve this for us. I have lived my intellectual life either directly or indirectly under the influence of perhaps the world's foremost scholar and proponent of the subjective economics, Lord Lionel Robbins. I recall winning no arguments and I know I lost many. The subjective economics cannot be *argued* with, any more than the Aristotelian philosophy that dominated all avenues of thought in the 16th century could be argued with. Aristotle's "means-ends" interpretation of all nature was no more vulnerable to rhetorical assault than is Robbins' means-ends economics. Both, however, are vulnerable to facts. Galileo's demonstration of the free fall law was the tiny pebble that shattered the magnificent crystal spheres of Aristotle. My discoveries about the facts that actually exist in the Toronto Stock Exchange are the tiny pebble that shatters the crystal-pure reasoning of the Subjectivists. They cannot explain those facts. Objective Economics, which is absolutely free of decision-making man, can explain them. The point is developed in my second chapter, "Unfreedom as an Economic Fact". I owe the awkward word "unfreedom" to Frank H. Knight, a giant like Lionel Robbins, but a giant who, also like Robbins, is steeped in the sin of an irrelevant "science".

Although the dispute of the second chapter comes from the technical literature of economics in the west, the issue involves all mankind. The relevant question is whether or not it is *useful* to interpret the economy we see around us as a manifestation of decision-making man, of man who has ends to his behavior, and, using the limited means at his disposal, tries his best to achieve those ends. In the west, economists and non-economists alike will answer that question, almost without thinking, in the affirmative. For them, decision-making man is at the centre. Their world is indeed "egocentric". The scientific answer, however, is not to be found in man's powers of introspection and rationalization, but in the facts that surround him. It has nothing to do with whether or not man *is* "free" in some philosophical sense and it has even less to do, if that were possible, with whether or not man *should be* free. It is purely a matter of what structures exist and whether or not a given point of view explains them adequately. In Chapter 2 we find that structures we have not perceived, largely because we centre all our thoughts on decision-making man, do exist, and decision-making man is totally inadequate to explain them. We have no alternative, therefore, but to say, as did Galileo, "there is a law...", and those who have grasped my previous book will know what that law is.

The same stock market study is used in Part IV to contest the interpretation the Marx-Lenin-Mao tradition places on society's "surplus value". On the one hand, we discover surplus value and even quantify it. This dignifies Marx and puts scientific teeth in his intuition. Because we *discover* it, however, we are able, on the other hand, to demonstrate that no theory of exploitation follows from it. This draws one of Marx's two incisors. In that same part, we are also able to discover, partly from the stock market data, but mainly from the principles of Objective Economics, that the so-called "law of contradictions" that underlies the communist doctrine of class struggle is grossly in error. *Economic life is not shaped by competition and suppression.* It derives from the intermediation that transposes illiquidity and liquidity, one into the other. "Illiquidity", as the word implies, is the opposite of "liquidity", although both must partake of the same "substance" since the one can be transformed into the other, in very much the manner in which current physicists see physical mass and physical energy transformable into each other.

Illiquidity, the *inability* to sell debt or equity instruments, represents a "coiling-up" or a "queuing-up" of liquidity. If liquidity (the ability to sell debt or equity) is seen as the generated *savings* of entities, then illiquidity is clearly their *investment* and it is in turn reflected by retardation of supplies. This is one side of market "balance". Simultaneously, however, as entities coil up their liquidity in investment, they also generate liquidity through production and sale. This is the other side of market balance, and that market balance is consistent with the economic state of the entities.

Unfortunately, Marx interpreted liquidity, which is the *dynamic working capital* of entities just as it is their *generated savings*, as an exploitative "surplus value". Instead of being exploitative or even a surplus, it is simply a manifestation that economies, or more correctly, the entities within them, are dynamic, are "growing from within" as their investment uncoils. It is because both liquidity (savings) and illiquidity (investment) are finally freed from subjective connotations that Objective Economics removes Marx's other incisor. We thus obtain much mileage from our stock market study. Given its findings and the principles of Objective Economics it confirms, we can detail, in Parts II and III, the "slavery to inflation" that has followed from the failure of the subjective economics of the west.

The gross immorality of the "moral suasion" that central banks currently carry out to maintain governmental insolvency (the "forcing" I mentioned before) is perhaps the most traumatic discovery in this woeful tale. It leads, in my final chapter, to the conclusion: that dismantling central banks, at least until their governments are solvent, is the condition of survival.

The final division of the work, Part V, then, is the politics of passive resistance to insolvent governments; passive, as I said before, in order to sustain the tradition of human liberty. The goal is to perform for insolvent governments the role that private banks would have played had they not been subverted from their function by central banks. It consists in withholding credit from insolvent customers, namely governments.

This role has been thrust upon the public by policies honestly, but erroneously, designed for its benefit. In short, it must rescue governments from the folly of economists.

CHAPTER 2

"Unfreedom" As A Fact

A. Introduction

In this chapter I shall use data yielded by a study of the balance sheets of the 300^5 companies included in the Toronto Stock Exchange composite index to demonstrate that the economic state of companies can in no useful scientific sense be related to choice. Whatever the "ends" of business behavior, and whatever the limitations placed on realization of those ends by the available "means", the data configurations we discover are not consistent with any calculus relating the two. They are, to the contrary, *consistent with theorems developed in the new and natural science of Objective Economics*, some of which will be described in this chapter.

That this demonstration refutes and reduces to "mere raving" the assertions of relevance of today's economics of the west, cannot be better admitted or expressed than in the following statement of apology that we owe to the leading economist and philosopher, Frank H. Knight:

"If, at a minimum, the concepts of desire and satisfaction, end (in a personal sense), and achievement of end, are not 'real' or 'objective' in the sense of being valid units of discourse, then the whole content of economics, technology and all practical discussion whatever is illusion, and the discussion itself is without meaning, mere raving. That this is not true is as certain as any assertion whatever — *at least* as certain as any assertion regarding those external physical objects which are the subject matter of the physical sciences. The conclusion in regard to the status of the notions of desire and satisfaction does not need to be put in words."[6]

If the means-ends calculus, which is to say the "notions of desire and satisfaction", is so profound an intuition of economic activity that its status "does not need to be put in words" and is "*at least* as certain as ... the subject matter of the physical sciences", then we should at least be able to see the working of the economic laws as we do physical laws. If, as we shall find, we not only fail to see them working, but see something else, namely natural laws, then the time has come to put the little toy bugles and tin drums of modern economics on the nursery shelf, and move to a larger bedroom.

It is true that economists have developed a discipline out of the means-ends calculus. It merely explains in great and rigorous detail, however, the strict implications of what most people believe. The interpretation of our own acts and those of others is made, almost universally, in terms of "choice" acting under restraints of various magnitudes. Laymen think and talk that way. Columnists write that way. Businessmen and leaders in society and government explain what they have done that way. My demonstration, therefore, while reducing modern economics to "mere raving", also challenges the fundamental thought form of people in general.[7]

The whole issue has nothing to do with the metaphysical question of freedom of the will. Knight points this out in the reference cited.[8] The issue is not whether our wills are free, nor even whether what we say we choose really comes about as a result of choosing. The essence of my argument is that reality, scientific reality, is what the natural science of Objective Economics demonstrates it to be. Let us move to some examples.

B.   The Relevance of the Debt Structure Ratio

Central to Objective Economics is what I call the debt structure ratio.

It is a measure of the relationship between an entity's total receivables and its total payables. "Entity" refers usually to a company or corporation, small or large, but it applies equally to families, individuals, or governments. For example, in June 19-- the Smith family's income was $2,250. During the month it paid out $2,000 for food, housing, clothing, transportation, taxes and recreation. Its receivables totalled $2,250, its payables $2,000, and the debt structure ratio was 1.125.

That, of course, is an oversimplification. The debt structure ratio varies from day to day as the Smiths' bank account deals with the bills. There is an additional time element in the fact that some payments to the Smiths (vacation pay, retroactive pay after raises, income tax refunds, etc.) are spread out, while payments by them (credit card account, post-dated cheques for heating, cable T.V. etc.) are spread out as well. Nevertheless it is clear that the Smiths' debt structure ratio bears a distinct relationship to how and when it pays the bills.

Here we are assuming that the Smith family, like the great majority of families everywhere, meets its obligations. Indeed, underlying Objective Economics is the basic assumption that it is inconceivable that obligations are not met since even if the debtor does not meet them, the creditor does. Further, Objective Economics refuses to believe in magic. It refuses to believe that the moneys required for obligations to be met are created by some mysterious process in which receivables and payables are not somehow linked. Sensible as this assumption may be, it is unfortunately true that our perceptions of governments as economic entities are not truly free from such magical implications. Of this more, much more, will be said subsequently.

Let us introduce a more rigorous concept of how the debt structure ratio relates to the patchwork of receipts and payments. For convenience, we will call the patterns they form "spectra".

Someplace in nearly all companies you will find two employees or two groups of employees who perform a very boring activity. One opens the mail, takes the cheques out of it that pay bills to the company, and attaches to those cheques the invoices they pay. The other writes cheques to pay bills, and attaches to those cheques the invoices they pay. In small companies a single employee, even the "boss" may perform both functions. Whatever the size of the company, the activity is essentially the same as in the Smith family.

In some companies, probably most, a further step is taken. Not only are incoming cheques attached to the invoices they pay, but a note is taken of how long the invoice has been outstanding. A similar note is made regarding outgoing cheques. This again, though more formalized, is what the Smith family does. For both incoming and outgoing cheques, therefore, it is possible to prepare "spectra" that say, in summary that

"*as* Company A paid bills of $1,000, it received payments *for* bills that had been owing up to

0 (cash sales) — $	100
10 days —	200
up to 30 days —	500
up to 60 days —	1,100
up to over 60 days —	1,500

or

"*as* it was paid bills of $1,000, it paid bills that had been owing up to

0 (cash purchases) — $	85
10 days —	100
up to 30 days —	300
up to 60 days —	800
up to over 60 days —	1,200."

In these two spectra there is no simple relationship between the $1,500 and the $1,200 since *being paid* bills of $1,000 (the first case) is not necessarily concomitant with *paying* bills of $1,000 (the second case).

That these two spectra can be constructed, and often are, is not to be questioned. Now consider two different "states" of the same company. In the first case, and at a particular time, we assume that in total it is owed $1,000,000 and owes $500,000. In the second case, and at a different time, it is owed $500,000 and owes $1,000,000. Thus, in the first case, the ratio of its total receivables to its total payables (its "debt structure ratio") is 2, whereas in the second it is .5. We assert:

Theorem I:

It is absolutely evident that if economies work in such a manner that obligations are met, then the succession of spectra that will be observed for the first case will differ markedly from the succession of spectra of the second case.

Corollary I-A

From this it follows that *the spectra of payments, in and out, depend, in some manner, upon the debt structure ratio.*

Within the spectra of payments, in and out, there frequently are receipts for sale of immature paper (promises to pay at some future time) such as buyer notes, and there frequently are payments for purchase of immature paper (buying, or "discounting", someone else's promise to pay). Sometimes also, the receipt for an immature piece of paper that is sold is another immature piece of paper that may have shorter or longer maturity. Similarly what is given for an immature note that is purchased is sometimes another immature note that may have shorter or longer maturity. Let us call these activities "intermediation".

It goes without saying that the configuration of intermediation will be different when the company's debt structure ratio is 2, than it will be when the debt structure ratio is .5. We can thus state:

Theorem II:

It is absolutely evident that if obligations are to be met, the pattern of a succession of intermediation activities that will be observed if the debt structure ratio is 2, will be different than that observed if the debt structure ratio is .5.

From this follows:

Corollary II-A

The pattern of intermediation activities depends upon the debt structure ratio.

And from Theorems I and II, we assert:

Theorem III:

The pattern of relation between the spectra of in and out payments and the configuration of intermediation activities, depends upon the debt structure ratio.

The simplicity of these three theorems and their two corollaries leads us to put them to the test. We do this by examining a large number of companies to determine whether the debt structure ratio is an important classificatory tool with which to approach the economy. If we find that it is such a tool, we have of course not proven that other ways of classifying economic acts, such as the means-ends calculus, are *not* important tools. If, however, we find that the classification of economic acts delivered by the debt structure ratio stands on its own in a manner inviting scientific interpretation not tied to decision-making man, the case for means-ends, which has only been asserted, never proved, will be weakened, if not destroyed.

First let us see how debt structure ratios work as a classificatory principle. To do this, we measure, from the balance sheets of a large number of companies, their debt structure ratios. We then will count the number of occurrences of debt structure ratios in small ranges. That count will show us whether or not the economy so works that there appear to be "grooves", as it were, in the continuum of debt structure ratios into which companies seem to confirm themselves.

Accordingly, we calculated the debt structure ratios from the balance sheets of the companies included in the composite index of 300 companies in the Toronto Stock Exchange. In all, 273 balance sheets were usable and were examined for the most part for the seven years from 1973 to 1979. In total, 1928 debt structure ratios were measured, 108 of them prior to 1973 but subsequent to 1968, and the balance, 1820, being 1973 or later.

Given the variety of businesses involved, and the variety of people involved in managing those businesses, we might expect the values of those debt structure ratios to be dispersed very widely over a range from close to zero up to almost any number. In fact, whether looked at from the viewpoint of the man in the street or that of the subjective economist, the debt structure ratios are, at best, incidents in the achievement of the alleged ends of the business. Debts (payables) may be large or small compared with what is owed to the business (receivables). Because the assumed or alleged ends of the business vary as widely as the means their owners and managers adopt to achieve them, the debt structure ratios (total receivables/total payables) might be expected to vary just as widely.

Considering the range of debt structure ratios from zero up to 10, for example, there are 10 sub-ranges of .1 from zero up to 1, 10 more from 1 to 2, so that up to a value of 10 we have 100 subranges of .1. Similarly, since there is no reason debt structure ratios cannot be as high as any pre-selected number, we can as well raise our limit from 10 to 1000. If we do that, then there are 100 x 10 x 10 subranges of .1 up to 1000. Our commonsense tells us, *chiefly by default of reasons not to believe so*, that actual debt structure ratios could be found with almost equal chances in any one of those sub-ranges. We might expect some central tendency, some clustering around some part of the whole range because we see such central tendencies in all walks of life, but where that clustering should be expected to appear, above or below a debt structure ratio of 1, above or below one valued at 2, and so on, is very difficult to guess.

Fortunately we do not need to guess since we have made the measures and can add up how many occurrences of debt structure ratios there are in each subrange. This array of frequencies is shown in Appendix I for sub-ranges of .1 in the debt structure ratio. In summary, 90% of all measures were less than 3.50, 75% of all were less than 1.70, 66% of all were less than 1.30, and 53% of all were less than 1.10. In short, rather than debt structure ratios having almost any value, occurring in almost any range, the 35 sub-ranges of .1 from 0 to 3.50 in the 100 such sub-ranges up to 10 contained 90% of them, the 17 sub-ranges up to 1.70 contained 75% of them and so on.

Further, certain individual sub-ranges of .1—specifically, that containing debt structure ratios close to 1, that containing ratios close to .82, and that containing ratios close to .69—contained the three largest frequencies of all sub-ranges. Fully 10% of our cases were in the sub-range around 1, more than 7% were in the sub-range around .82, and more than 6% were in the sub-range around .69, i.e., 23% of all cases were in these three sub-ranges alone. As is shown in the charts in Appendix I, even when we examine the data by individual years, these relations vary only marginally.

What do we learn from this extremely laborious study? It seems that whatever economists allege businessmen are doing, trying to maximize profits, to retain control, to satisfy ends of behavior even more esoteric than these, there are remarkable tendencies for large numbers of them to end up running companies that have the problems associated with a very few debt structure ratios. Obviously, we are dealing with central tendencies, *invisible hands at work*, that shape the whole of our reality under study in a particular way. Further, although there are changes, year to year, they appear to affect our major modalities only slightly. In short, if it is useful to see man as a decision maker on the grounds that reality is alleged to reflect those decisions, man, as a single man or as a group, would appear to exhibit very little of the variety with which he is credited.

An a priori case exists, therefore, that *unfreedom* or determination by some overvailing law, is a basic fact of economic reality. To press this case further so that it can be brought before the courts, we must now demonstrate that whereas man, interpreted as a decision maker who pursues his ends as well as his means allow him, does not explain the facts of these charts, Objective Economics does explain them. I propose to make this demonstration by introducing three of the important, albeit abstract, quantities that are developed in Objective Economics. One quantity is called the "generated savings" of the entity. The second quantity is called its "investment". The third quantity is what is called the "leverage" of the entity. This quantity is the measure of the ability of the entity to reborrow what it has loaned, *as it has loaned it.*[9] That activity is extremely familiar to us, on a moment's reflection, because when a bank lends us money, it does so by *borrowing it back*, since it "opens a deposit" for us with the loan, which is to say, *we* lend the loan back to the bank. Since these acts by the bank are virtually simultaneous, they exemplify the activity at its peak. Consequently we should expect banks to have a debt structure ratio that yields maximum leverage. That is indeed the case; they have ratios very close to unity, which is the debt structure ratio yielding maximum leverage as it is defined.

In Appendix II, I explain how to calculate these quantities from the balance sheet of the entity. For the present purposes our interest is in their relationship with the debt structure ratio. This is shown in the chart accompanying Appendix II.

Each of these quantities is rigorously defined in Objective Economics and in many respects understanding what that science has to tell us about inflation is a matter of understanding what they are and how they interrelate. For the purposes of this chapter, however, their significance is that they explain why debt structure ratios cluster around the points mentioned before, namely 1, .82, and .69. At each of those ratios *our three quantities have unique optimal values*. For a ratio of unity, leverage is at its *maximum* for a given sum of total receivables (R) and total payables (P). For a ratio of .82, investment is at its *minimum*, no matter what the sum R + P. For a ratio of .69, generated savings is at its *minimum*, again, as for leverage, for a given sum R + P.[10] Thus we see that whereas the subjective economics tells us nothing about why reality is shaped the way it is, Objective Economics, via these three quantities, tells us a great deal. In fact, we can simplify our thought forms by describing maximum leverage, minimum investment and minimum generated savings as three circumstances defining "least economic energy". The tendency for entities to cluster in those circumstances, therefore, can be described as a tendency for entities to "fall to" or "rise to" the circumstance of least economic energy. This is what I call the "law of constrained fall to states of least economic energy".[11] Economists have failed to discover this natural law of all economic activity. They have in fact confused its manifestations in the real world, despite Adam Smith's poetic reference to an "invisible hand" as early as the 18th century, with alleged attempts of *entities* to maximize or minimize certain "variables" that are subjectively conceived. Because they have conceived the economy as made up of individual "maximizers", as distinct from seeing the system as "economizing", they have approached the problem of inflation with tools that were peculiarly useless in helping them understand how it is caused. Of this, more later.

In general, entities have considerable ability to *engineer* their activities in such a manner that they can swim upstream against the law of constrained fall just as man has learned how, despite a law of gravity that almost precludes it, to get an airplane off the ground. There are borders that cannot be crossed, however, in such endeavors, without the evidences of inflation emerging. That fact also finds a parallel in the physical world because if our energy input is too great in swimming against natural law, we encounter phenomena of fission or fusion that are self-sustaining and strangely dangerous. Modern man, we shall find, through his governments, which have acted out the follies of the subjective economics, has broken such barriers. As we shall see, inflation is the result.

From the chart of Appendix II, we find that these "barriers" are in actuality ranges of the debt structure ratio around the ratios yielding minima of generated savings and investment and the maximum of leverage. Within those ranges, the quantities remain nearly constant, which is to say, "conserved".[12-13] Thinking of 2½% variation from the minimum or maximum values as the limit of this conservation, investment is conserved for debt structure ratios from .70 to 1.0, generated savings is conserved for ratios from .50 to 1.0, and leverage is conserved for ratios from .75 to 1.40.[14-15] Our measures of all debt structure ratios reveal that 56% of all 1928 occurrences lies between .50 and 1.40, a range containing only 9 sub-ranges of .1!

These facts tell only the story as it relates to the debt structure ratio occurrences. They tell us where, i.e. in which ranges of those ratios, the companies exist, each company and each measured ratio counting as one. We obtain further insight to the remarkable "pull" of the law of constrained fall if we calculate, and add up, the net worth[16] of each company falling in each sub-range.

From the TSE300 Study we discover that whereas 56% of our debt structure ratio occurrences fell in the range of ratios from .50 to 1.40, 68% of the net worth of our 273 companies fell there too. If we add our calculation of the generated savings for each company to its net worth, then we find that 70% of that sum lies in this range of overlapping conservations. Finally, we find that over 95% of the total leverage of those companies lies in that range. In short, the tendency for entities to constrained fall to a range of "least economic energy"[17] is powerful indeed. In fact it is so powerful that most of the occurrences lying outside this range of ratios from .50 to 1.40 can be "explained" by the newness of the entity (ratios less than .50), the fact the entity is a spin-off or subsidiary of another entity (more than 1.40), and similar considerations that suggest incomplete processes of adjustment. Clearly, constrained falling into the .50 to 1.40 range of debt structure ratios is what the economy is doing, what it always has been doing, and what it always will be doing. Without question, management pilots the ship and in so doing may well move the entity against the stream. When the hands are off, however, or even when they are slightly relaxed, the law of constrained fall takes over. It is the law of constrained fall that "economizing" is all about.

How to calculate generated savings, investment, and leverage is shown in Appendix II. Readers whose interest in economics is professional will wish to examine those methods and relate them back to their source in *How* ALL *Economies Work*. For the purposes of the literal arguments of this book, however, there are certain properties of these three quantities we should emphasize in the body of the text having grasped that all three, in their full quantitative rigor, are implied by the debt structure ratio and its two components, total receivables and payables.

Taking each of the three quantities in turn, savings referred to as generated savings have nothing whatever to do with an "act of saving" that requires a decision. Whether the entity is a Rothschild or a pauper, as long as the ratio of what is owed to it to what it owes is the same in both cases, its generated savings *per dollar of the sum of its receivables and payables* will be the same. This is so because generated savings of that specific amount is a *natural* and *necessary* and *sufficient* condition for that debt structure ratio to remain what it is, forever.

About the closest we can come intuitively to such a concept and quantity is "working capital". All businessmen know that having the physical wherewithal to produce and sell a product is not enough. Working capital is required, and as it is used "to work" the capital, it tends to replenish itself. To take a simple example, money is borrowed against the security of an existing facility in order to expand it. The debt is serviced out of increased revenue from the expanded facility; it is "self-liquidating". We can carry the analogy a step further by recognizing that businessmen also know that their requirement for what they call working capital tends to rise as the amount of debt they have to service rises. This is like saying that even working capital in that familiar sense tends to be related to the debt structure ratio and not to some decision-making process.

The analogy of generated savings to working capital is so intuitive that in earlier versions of the present text I actually used the expression "*dynamic* working capital" for what I now call, following Blackman (see note 9), generated savings. However, that required me to describe what I now call investment as "non-dynamic working capital". I think investment is a better term and since a good deal of the literature of economics relates savings and investment (Keynesianism), or the demand for money and investment (Friedmanism or Monetarism), I have stayed with the terminology of generated savings.

One of the peculiarities of the generated savings calculation from the balance sheet is that although its accurate calculation requires reference to four specific numerical constants that are deduced from first principles for each debt structure ratio, it always works out that if that ratio is in our conservation range, then generated savings is very close to 2% of the sum of total receivables and payables. Thus, with some experience, we can eyeball a balance sheet, add up those two totals, add them together, and by taking 2% of that total, estimate generated savings with considerable accuracy.

It will be seen in Appendix II that investment depends upon generated savings. In fact, it is simply this latter quantity, "balanced" (in a sense of pivot balance) over total receivables and total payables. As receivables rise relative to payables a queuing-up phenomenon develops so that investment increase really represents a *retardation*, or a slowing down, of generated savings. As we saw earlier (page 14), the transformation of generated savings into investment reduces liquidity because the savings are "tied up". At the same time, the act of investment generates liquidity through production and sale.[18]

Our third quantity, leverage, is in a sense the mirror image of investment. Leverage increases as the investment retardation of generated savings is less and decreases as that retardation is more. Entities that consistently retain near unity debt structure ratios ("banks")[19] exist almost entirely on working capital by which I mean that their borrowings (deposits) finance their loans, and their loans are made *by* borrowing, i.e. they "open deposits" with them. Their leverage is maximal, all other debt structure ratios, higher *or* lower, yielding less leverage.

Our three quantities, then, make it possible for economic work to be done. Perhaps their most exciting property is that they all have extremum values at somewhat different debt structure ratios. Many consequences follow from this, several of which are germane to later parts of our argument.

The modality of economic activity in which these three parts of the law of constrained fall resolve their differences is the intermediation (buys and sells) of immature paper and the international exchange of currencies. It is not the modalities of competition and suppression, as alleged by the Marxists and conceded by the subjectivists. In a general way, as a result of the universality of intermediation, there is always some entity "willing" to "help" any other solvent entity out simply because the law of constrained fall forces that conclusion on us. For an *insolvent* entity (which is to say, one that is markedly and repetitively outside the conservation range) to obtain such assistance, however, it must find a way to "trick" the economy, i.e. violate its conservation principles. Part of the results of such subversion is a depreciation of the currency and the accompanying manifestations of inflation. How central banks were able to perform such feats for their insolvent governments will concern us, indeed preoccupy us, in Parts II and III.

To conclude this chapter, I emphasize that the discoveries we have summarized thus far knock into a cocked hat more than a century and a quarter of economic thought of the western world. They do the same for communist economic thought for roughly the same period, but of that more will be said in Part IV. Let me make sure I have communicated as to the economics of the west, even at the risk of laboring a point.

The reader, and indeed all mankind, is faced with two ways of interpreting the economy. One way, the way I have called the "subjective economics", interprets data manifestations such as sales, prices, savings, investments, and so on, as the result of decision-making processes of people. All of us believe we are aware of such processes going on in ourselves and other people. It is from this interpretation of economic activity that we obtain the concept of a means-end economy, in which we see all economic activity as the result of our attempt to satisfy the ends of our behavior as best we can with the means at our disposal. Perhaps the "money supply" watchers are most typical of this genre.

A second way to interpret the data manifestations of the economy is to see them as the result of laws at work with which people, whether viewed as decision makers or not, have nothing to do. Such laws, therefore, would be *natural* just as physical laws are natural. Just as with physical law, people may very well *use* those laws to engineer their bit of the economy, perhaps even intuitively, without knowing what they are; nevertheless, the laws exist and compel.

Some economists have endeavored to use statistical regularities as if they were natural laws. The German "historical school" is a case in point, and the current return some writers have made to "long cycles" as of fundamental importance reflects the same spirit. This approach is *not* what I am talking about. Objective Economics, quite independently of data configurations of the real world, discovers natural laws that must hold:

(a) if obligations are to be met, i.e. if debts are to be paid back, if only by the creditor; and

(b) if all dollars that "disappear" by discounting "appear" by accumulation.

That "disappearance" and "appearance" refers to a balance in the sense of "equal and opposite" that must always exist in the economy between implicit and/or explicit discounting of immature paper, and its implicit and/or explicit accumulation. It is in this sense that Objective Economics may be said to accept Aristotle's dictum that money is barren, or more specifically in his words, "money born of money" is "most contrary to nature".[20]

The scientific laws that follow from these two assumptions are neither statistical regularities nor laws following from assumptions about decision-making man. They are *natural* laws that must hold if the economy is to be commensurable, i.e. if we can apply arithmetic to it.[21] They are, in fact, the necessary and sufficient preconditions for an economic arithmetic to be possible that will allow both past and future to be connected with today's facts.

What the results of the stock market study show us is that companies in the market behave in a certain way as seen by those natural laws. Instead of "moving" to special circumstances such as maximized profits, minimized costs, or whatever the implications of a decision-making point of view indicate, they in fact move to *special circumstances of our laws*. In particular, they tend to cluster at debt structure ratios at which both generated savings and investment tend to be least and leverage tends to be most. To say that they are *trying* to do this, when they in fact *are* doing it, is totally unnecessary. In fact, in no relevant scientific sense are they *trying* to do anything. Even if they are moving to maximized profit or whatever goals are consistent with the subjective economics, we do not "see" them do this. What we see is something quite different. They are simply responding to the invisible hand of natural law as it works its way through the intermediation going on in the economy.

As we enter into the sad story of how the prevalent theory of subjective economics entrapped most of the world into the slavery of inflation, it is fundamental to realize that these data, scant as they are, dismiss that theory from an understanding of how economies work. That dismissal of course includes both the central core of the discipline, which is the subjective theory of value, and its derivative macroeconomics. Notions such as gross national product (GNP), gross national expenditure (GNE), balance of payments (BOP), money supply (M_1, M_{1A}, M_2, etc.), personal income (PI), the consumer price index (CPI), etc., all fall casualty to the same demonstration, for these are all concepts which attempt to model an economy that is thought to work in terms of decision making.

It is almost with a sense of outrage that economists and nearly every type of commentator on the economy hear that they must give up their macroeconomic aggregates, for they have become (since the Keynesian folly of 1936)[22] the very fabric of their lives. Concepts such as the addition of all produced goods and services, however complex that aggregation may be to yield Gross National Product (GNP), concepts which totally ignore the debt structure ratios of entities, are manifest absurdities once we know, as we now do know, that those ratios are an absolutely fundamental part of the workings of economic law. On to the same garbage heap must go "money supply"[23] which our central bankers supposedly currently keep within the sharp focus of their beady eyes when they are not looking at the equally foolish measure, *the* rate of interest. Surely this—the delusion that such intellectual garbage can be used to formulate policy—is the most astonishing of all the sad array of "facts" describing the intrusion of the wrong, wrong, wrong, subjective economics to modern society.

The demise of belief of relevance of these concepts is a trauma many will not survive because, as I have said, they have become part of the fabric of their lives. Not only do economists spend billions of taxpayer money, both collecting and using them, but politicians, commentators, and the general public spew them forth as from a Gatling gun. Without them, economists and many others would be speechless; our "law of constrained fall" cuts the economists from the body of economic understanding as a cancer is cut from the living body.

Even though many will not survive the surgery, there is a gain. The gain is understanding what inflation is and how it occurs as soon as any economy attempts to retain, and maintain within it, a major insolvency. That this insolvency which has been retained and maintained is governmental, and that it has caused and is causing inflation, will be demonstrated in Parts II and III.

PART II

THE SLAVERY TO INFLATION

CHAPTER 3

The Pathology of Insolvency

When Karl Marx published the Communist Manifesto in 1848 and wrote its final words,

> "The proletarians have nothing to lose but their chains. They have a world to win. Workingmen of all countries unite!"

there still *were* "proletarians" in chains. In fact, at that time Joseph Stalin's father was a chattel in the Russian province of Georgia where he was viewed by Tsarist law as attached to the land of its (and his) owner. Slavery, in short, was real. Because of that reality, Marx aroused a very deep sympathy in those fortunate enough to be workingmen and he created burning enthusiasm in an intelligentsia that was willing to lead them.

Man's slavery to inflation is no less real than the chains to which Marx pointed. Our ability, whether workingmen or intelligentsia, to call up deep sympathy about it, however, is much less real. Many people feel they gain from inflation or at least are uncertain as to whether they do or do not. Since it is associated with removing much of the highly visible poverty in modern societies, it has tended to become cocktail circuit talk somewhat like the weather or the common cold. Of course, we can go slumming by visiting Third World countries or ghettos of large cities, but even when we do that we have our defences up and are almost as ready to blame the inhabitants for their plight as we are to sympathize with them. Ironically, the real outrage at inflation is often expressed by the most privileged members of society, who take care to protect themselves against its effects, and have the greatest competence to do so.

Despite all this difficulty in finding at whom we should be angry, or even *if* we should be angry, let us begin with the slavery aspect of inflation that I claim is as real as Marx's chains. Perhaps if we can understand that we all *are* slaves to inflation, the enemy will be identified in passing. Perhaps also if we find that even when the enemy is identified it is difficult to make our gorges rise, that may not be a bad thing. If the task of getting rid of our slavery is complex, cool heads and steady hands will almost certainly be required.

We learned something of extreme importance in the preceding chapter. We learned that the economy *as a system* has laws that transcend what we desire to do, laws that transcend those desires by making them harder to realize than if those laws did not exist. This is a familiar concept. Almost everyone at some time or another has wished that some natural physical law such as the law of gravity did not exist, perhaps when climbing the stairs after a hard day's work, or when lifting a heavy load. But it does exist and it often makes our lives very difficult. We now know that the same situation exists in the economy. We also know, however, from our technical arts, that the law of gravity is not all bad. Without it, for example, we should be unable to drop our collection in the plate at church. Perhaps we shall find that the same beneficence of nature is inherent in the economy's laws.

When we reflect upon what we learned in the last chapter and let our minds jump to the familiar modern event of a government spending more than it takes in in revenues ("deficit financing") as a way of its life, we come to two conclusions, one of them startling. The first conclusion is that repetitive deficit financing must imply a falling debt structure ratio. The second and startling conclusion is that once that ratio has fallen below about .69, the government is swimming *against* the mainstream of the economy's laws. We recall that such low debt structure ratio entities tend to be pushed or pulled, or both, into higher ratios. If the ratio continues to fall, however, as a result of successive deficits, that tendency is being resisted and defeated.

Let us be very clear about that fact. Assume that when deficit financing begins a government has been meeting its expenditure with taxes for a long time so that its debt structure ratio is likely near one to one. As it starts decreasing taxes relative to expenditure (or *increasing* expenditure relative to taxes—this is the route most governments have followed), although there will be some period over which the economy has to "get used to" its new modality, the fact the debt structure ratios of entities tend to rise or fall to around .82 (as well as 1) tells us that little resistance will be met. Such a government is still on nature's side, or at least nature works with it. Similarly, if its deficit financing persists, once its ratio has broken below .82 and the economy has become accustomed to it, the descent to .69 will also be aided and abetted by nature's law. Departing from .69 in a downward direction, however, is like heading into the open sea at the mouth of the St. Lawrence River. From your left comes the frigid sweep of Arctic waters rushing south; from your right, the warm streams flow north from the Gulf of Mexico. This is new and dangerous territory and it is highly speculative whether nature will help or hurt in any particular voyage.

How does nature reveal itself to an entity departed on such a voyage in the economy? The answer is familiar to all of us. The trading connections, by which I mean essentially in today's world the "banking connections", of the entity start to reveal what we can call a "tenseness". When its debt structure ratio was higher, its bank deposits came in relatively frequently compared with its withdrawals, whereas as its debt structure ratio continues to fall, it becomes clearer and clearer to the bank manager that he has to move fast indeed if he is to lend its deposits (which he of course borrows) before they are wiped out by withdrawals. Tenseness between the entity and its bank, as I say, comes more and more to characterize their relationship and that is a natural manifestation of the mounting inconsistency of what the entity is doing and what its bank is doing.[24]

I am, after all, talking about government and perhaps governments can avoid this tenseness that besets us lesser entities. Before we accept that premise, however, let us pursue the deficit financing even further and refresh our memories of how the system will treat us. Then let us back up and see just what special armament government brings to the battle.

A new depth of tenseness in the banking relationship develops when the ratio of what an entity is owed to what it owes has fallen to approximately .50. Down to .50 the problem being posed to the bank manager is rather like his starting out by receiving deposits from the entity on a Monday that are all used up as withdrawals by the next Monday, although some deposits trickle in during the intervening days. But then he finds that Monday's deposits slip to Tuesday, Tuesday's to Wednesday, etc., without any substantial change in the withdrawal pattern. As this happens, the bank manager notices something else. If one of the entity's suppliers is Bill Smith, the bank manager notices that the gap in time between when his customer deposits the money on which he will write a cheque to pay Bill Smith, and the time Bill presents it for cash, becomes shorter and shorter. In fact, it gets so short that just as the bank's customer is depositing the money to cover Bill's cheque, Bill comes in to cash it. In short, the day arrives, theoretically, in which the customer might just as well meet Bill for a drink and pay him then, thus cutting the bank out entirely.

Banks are not in the business of supplying meeting rooms to their depositors and the people to whom they write cheques. Therefore, as the bank manager notices the gap in time narrow, he asks himself a very interesting question. It goes something like this:

"Since my customer's money is hanging around shorter and shorter periods before it becomes Bill Smith's money, why do I not take a look at Bill Smith's banking connections and see if I can get them. If I can do that, then I do not care about my present customer's business because maybe my customer's money in Bill Smith's hands will hang around longer."

Now no general answer to the key question "will my customer's money in Bill Smith's hands hang around longer" can be given. Bill's affairs might be worse than those of the bank's present customer. A much less specific answer is available, and, as if guided by "an invisible hand", the bank manager accepts this answer and acts accordingly. The fact is, when the original customer's debt structure ratio has fallen to about .50, there absolutely must exist an "imaginary counter-entity" *defined by that customer* that has a debt structure ratio of $1/.50 = 2$, and that *does* in general have money that will hang around longer.[25] The notion of an imaginary counter-entity is not difficult to grasp. When I say that our entity is owed 50¢ for every dollar it owes, I say implicitly that there must exist some *group* of entities (one member of which is Bill Smith) that is owed $1.00 for every 50¢ *some other* group owes to the entity. Since the two groups are different, no *real* single entity is implied but what this means to the bank manager is simply that if he looks at a lot of Bill Smiths who are paid cheques by, and Tom Browns who pay cheques to, his customer, he will find that the majority of them do in fact have moneys that will hang around longer than that of his present customer.

Since a debt structure ratio of about .50 is an important point evoking a special response from nature, I think it is entitled to a special name. I call it the debt structure ratio at which the marketing efforts of the bank manager, i.e. his constant drive to obtain and hold new business, become "repolarized". His present customer is by no means a "dead beat" and he does seem to define some very exciting territory for searching for new depositors. Both for that reason, and also because his deposits still have a finite, if short, duration, the bank still wants his business. Is he worth buying lunch for? Probably not unless he is very large and can supply the bank manager with a great deal of useful information such as a detailed list of all his trading connections.

I do not wish to imply that when a deficit-financing government's ratio has fallen to .50, bells suddenly start to ring in the bank as if a burglary were in progress. The fact is, all the way from .69 down to .50, the bank manager has been becoming increasingly aware of a mounting problem. He may even start contacting a few of the Smiths and Browns. When .50 is reached, however, he can read his chequing flows just as clearly as a road map (subject to the information overload mentioned in Part III) and the message he receives, is

"start beating the bushes for the Smiths and Browns—we have a potential ringer on our hands."

Of course, bank managers do not speak that way publicly, especially about government, but there is a lot of difference between their public language and that of their internal memoranda.

CHAPTER 4

The Pathology of Insolvency— Repolarization of Bank Marketing

In this sketchy pathology of a declining debt structure ratio that follows from a persistent modality of deficit financing, we now have a problem. Whether a government spends more than it receives in taxes or not it finds great efficiency in dealing through the banks rather than by cash transactions. At a debt structure ratio of .50, however, it begins to forfeit the interest of its bank manager(s) in keeping its account(s), a problem of more and more severity as its ratio continues to fall. One way to handle that problem is to set up a type of business that specializes in moving money around, a sort of poor man's Brink's system, and paying its bills with "money orders" or whatever the particular "paper" of that business is called as distinct from paying them with cheques written on its bank account. This approach is very ancient in Northern Europe. By establishing such a system, or by direct cash payments for its bills (i.e. "cash" that it prints for the purpose), the government can continue to meet its obligations even though the banks do not find its deposits profitable unless they levy special service charges of one form or another.

In other words, on the surface at least, it appears to be able to live without the banks or to "subvert" the banking discipline by resorting to the printing presses.

But the recipients of those pieces of paper themselves open bank accounts with them. In short, the banks *borrow* them and relend them. Since those depositors are, in general, the components of the imaginary counter-entity of the increasingly insolvent government, the banks want those accounts because, in general, the funds in them hang around long enough that loans can be made out of them.

Now the banks present the money orders they accept as deposits for payment to the government. The government pays them with money, i.e. cash, which is a promise to pay money. Thus, both from whatever payments the government makes in cash and from "cashed in" money orders, the banks ultimately receive cash. The former they receive as deposits (bank borrowings) from government creditors. The latter they also receive as cash when they cash in the money orders. That cash, however, instead of being a *loan* to the bank, is a loan *to the government* because it honors its money orders by *promises to pay* (i.e. by dollar bills it prints).[26]

Thus we see that as the bank becomes less and less willing to *borrow* from the government (i.e. accept its deposits), it finds itself, via seeking the honoring of cashed-in money orders, more and more *lending* to government. This happens because it is a government liability that honors the money orders the banks have accepted from their recipients. This is indeed a strange situation. The bank is increasingly uninterested in *borrowing* from government because of the chequing flows it sees going through its bank account, flows that yield diminishing opportunity for the bank to make money by lending the balance of that account. Hence it seems highly unlikely that the bank will *lend* to that government, i.e. accept the government's money to honor the money orders it has issued. The reason this is so is that banks in fact lend by *opening deposits*, i.e. by immediately borrowing back what they lend. We already know, however, that the banks are increasingly uninterested in having government deposits.

How does this situation resolve itself? How do the laws in accordance with which economies work accommodate this set of circumstances that becomes more and more severe as the government's debt structure ratio falls? Why do the banks not refuse to accept the money orders as deposits in the first place, knowing full well that when they do accept them they will have to accept a government debt, i.e. lend to government, to cash them in, and, in thus lending, be forced to borrow that amount back as deposits and end up with a depositor they do not want?

This is a much more difficult question than is realized. It cannot be answered by saying that the government can force the transactions to go forward by declaring its money to be "legal tender". All that does is force entities to accept it for goods or services rendered. We are not talking about goods certainly, and if banks lived on the services they render, they would starve to death. We are talking about banks being willing to borrow and lend and, in fact, being willing to lend *by* borrowing. The mere fact that the counting unit is said in the law to be legal tender has nothing to do with whether they will or will not do it. Forget, therefore, the legal tender way out.

Forget also glowing phrases about "national interest", "supporting the credit of the nation", etc. Banks are responsible to their directors who are responsible to their shareholders. Whatever their nationalist sentiments, and we have no a priori reason to think they are anything but the loftiest, these are both legal and moral commitments far transcending other considerations. In the name of both legality and morality, why do the banks not stop the declining debt structure ratio of government as it sinks below .50, the point at which their interests lie elsewhere? How does it happen that there appears to be no end to the process of deficit financing?

We can understand the answer to this question by recognizing that banks in retaining debt structure ratios very close to unity, so that whatever they borrow they lend, and whatever they lend they borrow, deal in what we call "hard" and "soft" transactions.[27] A hard transaction is one in which banks borrow at, say, 18½%, and lend at 20½%. A soft transaction is one in which, by actually diminishing your account balance by a certain amount, they allow you to diminish *their* account balance in some other bank by the same amount. I shall use the term, "customer acceptance" for these soft transactions and "credit creation" for the hard transactions.

As the government's debt structure ratio falls and that of its imaginary counter-entity rises, there is a drying up of the loan market from the very entities from which the banks are most anxious to borrow (i.e. from which they are most anxious to "accept" deposits). The banks find that to retain a unit debt structure ratio they must start lending to foreign banks, i.e. they open deposits in foreign banks. Although the domestic depositors they wish to have (the government's imaginary counter-entity) want less and less to borrow, some of them want to buy abroad. Via customer acceptances, the banks *annihilate obligations*. By this I mean that when they write a soft transaction, they acquire an asset in the sense that they take that sum out of the depositor's account, but they create a liability *in exactly the same amount* because they now owe that customer that sum, usually out of a foreign bank account balance held by the domestic banks. The banks charge a small fee for performing this service, usually about ¼ of 1% of the sum involved.

The effect of these soft transactions that annihilate obligations[28] in the sense stated is that by the banks opening deposit accounts abroad as the government's debt structure ratio falls, the government can chart its way through the stormy waters from a ratio of .69 down to .50, and even farther than that. Even though the domestic bank loan market is drying up progressively, as long as foreign banks will borrow (accept the domestic bank deposits), by a progressive switch from hard to soft transactions,[29] the domestic banks will not reject the government customer.

But now we, or more correctly the government, encounter another problem. Foreign banks carry out *their* hard transactions in *their* local currency. When they accept (borrow) the deposits of our banks, therefore, they "convert" our dollars to theirs. What happens to this "rate of exchange", as our government's debt structure ratio continues to fall?

The study conducted among the 300 companies in the Toronto Stock Exchange composite index threw much light on this question by confirming an important hypothesis about how value is created. To understand what happens to the exchange rate we need to understand that confirmed hypothesis. (The reader will suspect, quite correctly, that if our banks keep on absorbing our government's dollars by soft transactions involving more and more lending to foreign banks, our "dollar will tend to fall". The problem we must address is *why* it will tend to fall and to answer that question we need a theory that works, about how values are determined.)[30]

Rather than pursuing this question of the determination of exchange rates, let me return to the slavery allegation. Now that we have our deficit-financing government's debt structure ratio down to .50 and still falling, are we already slaves to something that looks like Marx's chains? Certainly from .50 down to lower ratios the government is forcing a marked increase in the ratio of soft to hard transactions. That almost certainly causes a depreciation of the domestic currency; domestic importers are "hurt" since their imports cost more. On the other hand, exporters are "helped" because their prices in foreign currency fall. Yet neither is enslaved, because if they do not like the new circumstances they can make a variety of adjustments to minimize their effects or even gain from them. The only worrisome problem that is starting to look a bit like slavery is what is happening to the private banks. If they had wanted to increase their ratio of soft to hard transactions before deficit financing became the rule, presumably they would have done it. Now that that is the rule, they are forced to do it, or so it appears, or they will find themselves borrowing money they do not lend or borrowing money from a customer (the government) that they are increasingly unwilling to have as a customer. Are the private banks being enslaved in this sense that they are being forced to do what they do not want to do?

The beginning of such a case can be made. Our domestic banks have undoubtedly had all along both deposits *in* foreign banks and deposits *from* foreign banks. Although the value of the former in foreign currency falls as they increase their foreign deposits, the value of the latter in domestic currency rises. There thus is some tendency to a compensating effect not unlike that between importers and exporters. We must not forget, however, that the switch to soft transactions itself reflects a drying up of the domestic non-governmental loan market. As a result, there is little potential for converting deposits *from* foreign banks into domestic currency and expanding hard transactions domestically. Such transactions can only be expanded with the government, and the private banks are already finding the government to be at best an "uninteresting" customer.

One option that may be open to them that is not inconsistent with their banking modality is to buy gold rather than expand customer acceptances. The reason gold purchase does not affect their banking modality is that it carries near zero accumulated depreciation with it. If a bank effects that purchase for its depositors, therefore, it deducts the amount of the purchase from its depositors' accounts, thus diminishing bank liabilities. But in retaining the gold *for* the customers, it decreases its assets in the same amount. Such transactions, therefore, annihilate obligations just as customers' acceptances do.[31]

Again, however, had the banks wanted to buy gold they would have done so. Being forced to do it by the government modality of deficit financing smacks of enslavement. Thus we can see a pattern of enslavement starting to be built around the private banks. They are being forced to do things as a result of government policies, things they would not have done in all probability had those policies (deficit financing) not existed. Further, whereas importers and exporters can be said to be affected by those policies, they at least can and do change the import-export mix in their businesses and no clear case can be made that such changes do not leave them at least as well off. Banks, however, cannot be indifferent to being forced more and more into soft transactions. As with their services, if they had to live on what they are paid for them, they would starve to death.

CHAPTER 5

Some Principles of Banking

Let us look in some detail at why a *compulsion* exists upon the private banks. Banking is almost certainly the most delicate of the economic arts. Undoubtedly over all human history, thousands, perhaps millions of banks have flickered into view only to be snuffed out by departures, probably violent departures, from the banking modality. As stated in note 19, there are at least three criteria that must be met for a bank to exist. The first criterion is that it lends *by* borrowing and borrows *by* lending. If we could abstract away its original and subsequent equity inputs, that criterion implies a 1 to 1 debt structure ratio. Since we never can make such an abstraction completely, that ratio is always slightly higher.[32] Secondly, the ratio of accumulated depreciation to a bank's total receivables, as that total is defined in Objective Economics, must approach zero. This implies that its physical assets, as they wear out, do almost no economic work in the sense of affecting the net worth share of its balance sheet. In short, its "money does the work". Thirdly, mechanisms must exist virtually instantly whereby obligations it enters into *with* its customers that it cannot get rid of by obligations *of* its customers, can be annihilated. Customers' acceptances and, with some lapse in the 1945-1970 period,[33] gold transactions, have been the main mechanisms historically for this vital ability to annihilate obligations. A fourth *charac-teristic* of banks, if not a criterion of their existence which we shall discover when I have faced the problem of how values are determined, is that banks tend ever to "burn out". By this I mean that the portion their net worth is of their natural reserves against deposits waxes and wanes but tends to decrease. If net worth is not replenished by new equity sales, the banking function will become unstable and probably the bank will cease operation as its debt structure ratio approaches closer and closer to the "ideal" ratio.[34]

There are, then, three criteria that must be met for a bank to exist. Assuming they are met, Objective Economics allows us to deduce the theorem that banks as a system will always *find they have* a reserve against their total payables of just slightly under 8%.[35] I have chosen the words "find they have" carefully. Banks do not *keep* a reserve as economists allege. They lend every dollar they borrow and borrow every dollar they lend, *and/or* they annihilate obligations to be sure they do. In doing those things, they *find* they always have "on hand" about 8¢ for every dollar they owe.

That fact has nothing to do with prudence, or with the existence or non-existence of statutory reserves expropriated by central banks. In fact, banks cannot even "see" the reserve of 8¢ because it exists in three different forms. Part of it is the bank's net worth. A second part is its generated savings (which is almost exactly 2% of the sum of its total payables and receivables) from hard transactions, and the remainder is its generated savings from soft transactions. Banks can see none of these quantities in prospect any more than we can "see" physical energy in prospect. They are nevertheless real from the scientific point of view and as long as they retain their banking modality, they make up the total of about 8¢ for every dollar of payables.[36]

The nature of the enslavement of private banks by the succession of government deficits, therefore, is that if they are to *retain their nature* as banks, they *must* dump domestic currency into foreign banks as deposits, they *must* in so doing switch to soft transactions to a dictated degree, or they *must* use the gold option. In addition, in so far as they do not dump currency or buy gold, they must raise the interest rate on existing demand loans and hence "primes". Slavery in its human sense is also a proposition that says if you want to retain your nature as a human, if you want to eat, to breed, in short, to live, then do this or that. I think any logical difference between that slavery and that starting to be imposed on the private banks by the government deficit modality would be hair-splitting. As I say, we are starting to make our slavery case in the context of governmental deficit financing.

Quite aside from the fact the enslavement of banks is not nearly as evocative of emotion as is the enslavement of a Marxian proletariat, we really are only starting to make the case and have by no means made it. The fact is, if the interface is between government as a bank customer and the private banks, even though the banks will find themselves driven into more and more soft transactions as the government's debt structure ratio falls to .50, once it reaches .50, one aspect of the repolarization of their marketing thrust is that the banks will start to "ration" their government business. Given only that interface, the banks, in finding that their ability to borrow back what they have loaned and relend it (i.e. their leverage) is being threatened, will start increasing their lending rate to pay for the increased waiting they must do to be able to retain their banking mode of life.[37] This is an alternative course of action that tends to "reciprocate with" or "be in perturbation with" their switch to soft transactions. Thus, the switch to soft transactions that reflects an attempt to get *rid* of waiting entirely so that maximum leverage can be retained, tends to be "traded off" against increases in the private banks' lending rate that tend to increase their *reward* for waiting as their need to wait increases. By and large such increases affect the rate on existing demand loans first.

As long as the banks retain their maximum leverage, however, the retardation their investment places on their generated savings remains almost exactly constant since at a debt structure ratio near unity the conservation ranges discussed above are not violated. This implies that increases to bank lending rates (for example, their "prime rates" to preferred customers) tend to be imparted to bank borrowing rates with the result that the "spread" between them remains almost constant although it may rise and fall continually in small degrees.[38]. Additions to bank net worth, therefore, which follow from that spread (i.e. bank profits), tend to keep step with additions to generated savings which in turn keep step with bank deposits which are essentially the bank payables. In so far as that does not happen, soft transactions rise and do so at the expense of gains in net worth and ultimately of reduction in the spread between borrowing and lending rates of the banks. This reduced spread is largely the result of the lower generation of savings from soft transactions.

I am sorry we cannot avoid these intricacies in trying to bring out the nature of our slavery to inflation and they are not completed yet. It is absolutely vital, however, that we use the new science to bring into the sharpest light the running room that is left to modern society, and no more than that running room. To be able to do that, we must understand banking and in many respects we must understand it better than bankers do. The banking industry has the unhappy tendency to present itself either as an activity so complex that ordinary people cannot understand it (but at the same time alleging that ordinary people do not need to), or as so simple that many people are ashamed to ask questions. Perhaps some readers are so aware of that tendency that they will take vicarious pleasure as we track down the nature of the slavery to which banks have unwittingly subjected themselves. In any case, I shall proceed and hope the reader will not lose patience with the intricacies of the argument.

Thus far we have thought of the government meeting its deficits by printing money and money orders. As its debt structure ratio fell, things worked very well for a time. What it now notices, however, is that as it carries its debt structure ratio below .50, a considerable quantity of dollars is being exchanged for foreign currency by banks. When that is not happening the rates of interest the private banks are charging *and* paying start to rise. Indeed, the government probably will observe these phenomena closely enough to realize that the sale of domestic dollars (the switch to soft transactions) tends to ease off as the rates of interest rise, whereas the rise in the rates of interest starts to ease off as the switch to soft transactions starts to rise. This of course happens because all three quantities, bank net worth, bank generated savings from hard transactions, and bank generated savings from soft transactions, all total 8% of the total payables of the banks which is the natural reserve ratio thrust on banks by their banking modality. As bank total payables rise, generated savings from hard transactions always rise almost exactly proportionately. For the fixed 8% actual reserves to be retained, therefore, any increase in the net worth component (resulting from increased spread of rates) must be compensated by a decrease in soft transaction generated savings. Conversely, any increase in generated savings from soft transactions must be compensated by a decrease in the net worth component. Thus we see that the natural reserve ratio of banks is absolutely fundamental to our understanding of the relation between domestic rates of interest and the value of the domestic currency.[39]

We emerge from this discussion, therefore, not with the allegation that slavery of the banks already exists once the government's debt structure ratio has fallen to .50, but with the feeling that if that ratio can somehow be taken lower and the banks forced into complying, then either they and the public and the government will be enslaved with higher interest rates, or they and the public and the government will be enslaved by a sell-off of the domestic currency. The fact is, the halcyon days of the government being able to meet its deficits by printing money and money orders without meeting either of these "resistances" are gone.[40] In a sense, therefore, the years of boyish enthusiasm in which Keynesian thought justified government deficits have come to an end when a debt structure ratio of .50 is reached by the government. Now, the government faces an adult world in which there are two courses: either the deficits must cease and be replaced by surpluses; or a continuing fall in the debt structure ratio must be accompanied by rising interest rates acting reciprocally with sell-offs of the domestic currency. Further, as the government's debt structure ratio continues to fall, the swings upwards in the rate of interest and downwards in the currency rate of exchange start at progressively higher and lower bases respectively.

CHAPTER 6

The Birth of Central Banks

So far, I have not presented the government as a borrower except that in "cashing in" money orders the banks found that they were accepting a promise by the government to pay, i.e. the government was in fact a borrower in that transaction. I have also built no agency or agencies between the government and the private banks. In short I have described a direct interface, as it is for most of us in dealing with the banks.

As we know, for most modern governments this has not been historically true. Most have been borrowers in a far more general sense and most have had a "central bank" interfacing between them and the private banks for many years before their debt structure ratios hit .50. The form of the borrowing has been bonds or bills of varying maturity dates. Although the various central banks have had differences among them, many have been modelled upon the Bank of Canada or the Federal Reserve Board and its relation with members of the Federal Reserve System. Both owe a great deal to the modes of activity of the much older Bank of England. We have now to add the borrowing activities of government and central banks to our discussion.

First, allow me to say that if a government was not "selling" bonds and bills of varying maturities as its debt structure ratio fell to .50, i.e. "borrowing", and if it had not formed a central bank, it would quickly find that any further decline in that ratio would bring both courses of action to the forefront. The private banks are by no means the only lenders in society and indeed they are a most peculiar lender because they lend *by* borrowing. Pension funds, corporations with spare cash, private individuals and many types of institutions are potential lenders. In a very general sense, in fact, when a deficit-financing government has become very large in the economy, its low debt structure ratio implies that many of these potential lenders are created. Clearly, as the banks come more and more to reject the government as a customer and repolarize their marketing effort to the government's imaginary counter-entity, one would expect that they would meet the government trying also to borrow from the same source. Since borrowing on varying maturities is a more complicated activity than simply printing currency or money orders and paying bills with them, it would be remarkable if some specialized agency were not formed to carry out the government's non-bank borrowing. Such an agency would have some of the functions of a central bank.

On the surface, therefore, we might expect the government, when at a debt structure ratio bordering on .50 and meeting opposition or indifference from banks, simply to head for lenders who *were* available, perhaps forming a special agency to deal with them. In that way, it could obtain the loans to finance further deficits and to lower its debt structure ratio still more. It might even borrow abroad and use some or all of that borrowing to combat the sell-off of domestic currency its private banks were forced into in order to retain their banking modality (emanating from the 8% natural reserve ratio), a sell-off actually caused by the government's low debt structure ratio.

I will not say that these dreams have not been dreamt and that some governments have not even put them to the test. They are doomed to fail ultimately, however, for the very reason that even those potential lenders are bank customers. Because they are bank customers, the fact that they lend to the government involves bank withdrawals. As the government's debt structure ratio continues to fall, if it borrows from those desirable bank customers, those withdrawals speed up relative to the deposits of those customers. The lenders may remain very solvent, some even with very high debt structure ratios. Nevertheless the overall effect of their withdrawals (speeding up to supply funds to the government, funds the banks themselves will not supply without either raising rates or selling off domestic currency) is the same as if the banks had lent more to the government. In short, the natural reserves of the banks are protected by the interaction of increased rates of interest with increased soft transactions.

The only way this continuation of "more of the same" can be avoided is if the government can build between itself and the lenders, be they private banks or others, an institution that is itself a *bank* which, in its interface *between* government and lenders, *has its own mechanism for annihilating obligations*. If that can be achieved, then a whole new lease on the life of deficit financing can be assured. The government's debt structure ratio can be given a strong thrust downwards that the private banks cannot and do not control and must serve. Such an institution is a central bank.

I have purposely introduced central banks in the context of their being a solution to a problem in government financing that *already exists*. This has indeed been the case on more than one occasion, the most famous being the Bank of England which was born out of the bankrupting of London's goldsmiths (the "bankers" of the day) by the British Government late in the 17th century. The Federal Reserve System, which finally took specific shape by Act of Congress in 1915, was also born out of financial problems of the United States Federal Government, problems that were aggravated by the plethora of state banks and state banking laws. The Bank of Canada, however, although it emerged at a time of deep depression and currency problems (1934-5), did not inherit any specific or pressing problems in government debt raising. Indeed, as Prof. Blackman points out,[41] there was not much the Bank of Canada could do for several years after March 11, 1935, when it first opened its doors. Raising whatever money the government needed was neither its fundamental problem nor purpose since deficit financing was not the government modality.

I have chosen to present central banks in the crisis environment for governmental financing because it is only if we see them as an instrument *allowing* deficit financing to continue beyond the point at which the private banks would permit it that we can understand why central banks are not *inflation-fighters*. In actual fact *their very existence as banks is predicated on the existence and maintenance of inflation. Without it, there is no fundamental need for them*[42]. In short, were it not for inflation, central banks would do nothing for government or for the public that could not be achieved by private banks interfacing directly with government. Central banks are called into existence *to create* inflation. Inflation is the condition that governments with debt structure ratios falling below .50 require in order to meet their obligations. That is why mankind *and* governments are enslaved *by* inflation pari passu with the calling of central banks, *acting as banks*, into existence.

When I speak of central banks acting *as* banks I refer to them as institutions that not only borrow and lend money. I refer to them as institutions such that, when they borrow, they take a quick look to see if they can lend on hard transactions and if they cannot, they annihilate the obligation of the borrowing. It is this process of obligation annihilation that is the "pressure" downwards or inwards on credit creation that is the essence of banking as distinct from simply managing money. What distinguishes a *central* bank from private banks is the manner in which those obligations are annihilated.

We can fix this distinction in the method of annihilating obligations clearly in our minds if we think back a moment to the state of the governmental-private bank interface when the government's debt structure ratio is about .50. I have pointed out that at that state the banks are starting to look earnestly at other lenders (depositors) than the government. I have also pointed out that government itself probably looks to those lenders if it is borrowing; but unfortunately in so far as it does borrow from them, the change in their chequing flows acts against bank leverage just as would increased borrowing by the government from the banks. The dream of government, therefore, of saying, "if the banks don't want our business, we'll go elsewhere", is shattered. But there is one way out, crazy as it may sound. What if instead of putting those new potential lenders to government in the position of draining their bank accounts to lend to government, government, that is, the central bank, *lends them the money so that they can lend to it*? If that happens then the loan or some part of it is a liability of government but it is also an asset because even though it must pay the loan back, the loan must also be paid back to it. This is the essence of what is called in Canada the Purchase and Resale Agreement with a number of "designated brokers" who are called "money market dealers" in street language.

In applying this mechanism, the central bank actually expands the universe of lenders since it comes to the market equipped with newly printed money in a considerable degree, that degree depending upon how much it must lend so that it can borrow. This allows it to "edge" more and more of its debt into the economy. As it deposits the proceeds of its borrowing in the private banks, the chequing flows in those government accounts look better to the private banks. The resale part of the agreement with the brokers, however, has a very short term, conventionally for one day but often renewed for further days. This gives the broker only a short period in which to resell the paper he acquired by lending to the central bank. When he does resell it (at a slight mark-up) bank withdrawals do hit the private banks, withdrawals that are largely equated by deposits from the central bank of the proceeds of the loan.

Thus, through the annihilation of obligations carried on by the central bank there is a steady and insidious penetration of the private banks' total deposit structure by government with deposits those banks would reject or at least not seek if the central bank did not exist. In principle, this action of the central bank is very much as if you and I were somehow to force many bank depositors to withdraw their money from the banks and even though the banks did not want us as depositors because they knew from experience our money did not hang around very long, they accepted our deposits because they found they had loaned more money than they had borrowed. It is in a similar manner to this that private banks that would walk a country mile rather than accept depreciated money as deposits, in fact are forced to do so.

More specifically, the activity of the central bank is carried out in such a way that whereas private banks would not allow the government's debt structure ratio to keep on falling because the private banks' leverage would be threatened,[43] the central bank annihilation activity does allow that ratio to fall. By trading off falling exchange rates and rising interest rates, the central bank can make it look as if it is pursuing tight or easy money policies, the private banks being helpless to stop those phenomena and still continue to be banks.

It is almost a piece of mother wisdom of those who constantly complain about the printing of money by government that the mechanism involved is the purchase of government debt by the central bank with newly printed money. That mechanism, however, leaves us with no explanation of how the private banks are forced to accept that newly printed money as government deposits. To understand that acceptance we must introduce an annihilation mechanism that extends beyond the relations of the central bank with government. In Canada that mechanism is the Purchase and Resale Agreement. In the United States it is discounting of bills held by private banks by the Federal Reserve System. I emphasize the former in this book.

I shall return to this obligation annihilation mechanism that is associated with the crystallization of central banks out of the swirl of economic activity in a moment. This is a good place however to make a comment about the alleged logical and practical separation of monetary and fiscal policies.

Fiscal policy, as its title suggests, relates to the financial activity of government that creates its new payables and its new receivables. Its end product, therefore, is always the R, P and R/P, the debt structure ratio of government. As we have argued, if fiscal policy is such that deficits accumulate, this debt structure ratio falls. It is through fiscal policy that modern governments are alleged to reflect the desires of the people, desires that may include such items as health care, unemployment insurance, etc. Thus fiscal policy, so far as government is "representative", is the living embodiment of a great deal of our freedom.

Monetary policy, as its title suggests, relates to how the government, or its financial agents, handle money. It depends partly upon the operation of the government's own accounts, which is to say, paying its bills and relating the revenue it collects, mostly by taxation, to paying them. That part of monetary policy is largely determined by fiscal policy. For example, if fiscal policy creates a deficit, then monetary policy will be concerned with how the deficit will be financed, by printing money, borrowing money, or outright theft, which is to say, expropriation.[44]

Running the government's bill-paying activity is only part of what is usually meant by monetary policy. Just as fiscal policy reflects the desires of the people to have government do certain things, so monetary policy endeavors to reflect at least some of the desires of the people regarding money matters. Rising prices may be regarded as an evil, and monetary policies may be designed to combat them. Thus monetary policy, like fiscal policy, may appear to represent important freedoms held by individuals, in that case, the freedom from rising prices.

It is usually more difficult to justify or even to identify the relation of monetary policy with freedom than it is to justify and identify that relation for fiscal policy. The difficulty is perhaps typified by the fact that fiscal policy tends to involve the whole sweep of representational political activity whereas monetary policy is usually left under the control of an individual or a board that by law is not directly under political control. This implies that, to some degree, monetary policy is not part of the political process. The fact remains, however, that monetary policy is intended to be on the side of the people, and, in that sense, represents part of our freedom.[45]

It is basic to the manner in which subjective economists think about the economy that fiscal and monetary policies be logically and demonstrably separable. That is, the problem of meeting the obligations of government in consistency with the manner in which money "works" in the economy cannot be such that the government as a whole is totally preoccupied with it so that fiscal and monetary policy merge. In short, the assumption that fiscal and monetary policies are in fact logically and demonstrably separable implies either that money-issuing government is not insolvent or that it never can be insolvent. From the scientific point of view, the subjectivists are bound to equate these two alternatives because their discipline contains no principles or specific criteria of solvency or insolvency.

We have just brought ourselves to a stage in an argument at which we are saying that the economic state of government, which largely reflects *fiscal* policies, has created an economic climate for government that *requires* central banking if fiscal policy, which represents freedom, is to continue. That is, we have argued ourselves into a position whereby if fiscal policy is to continue, it can only do so if monetary policy can do certain things for it. Thus fiscal policy, which represents the bulk of our freedoms, has become the handmaiden of monetary policy. Further, we have found that this is a *natural* phenomenon which results from the economic state of government, i.e. from its debt structure ratio of .50. In short, at that state, if a government does not have a central bank, it will have to invent one if it wishes, through its fiscal policy, to continue deficit financing.

Thus, whatever distinction we have made between the freedoms represented by monetary policy and the freedoms represented by fiscal policy, no longer holds. Fiscal policy, which was driven to create central banks, has become their creature. Born of the desire to legitimize deficit financing, our central banks have made it a permanent condition of policy, and made us slaves to inflation in the process.

As we shall see, however, the disintegration of fiscal policy does not happen instantly. As government, assisted by its central bank, descends to debt structure ratios below .50, it still has a breathing space before fiscal policy becomes totally subservient to monetary policy, i.e. to the central bank.

CHAPTER 7

Central Banks' Role in Inflation

Let us return to the particular manner in which central banks annihilate obligations and thus pressure themselves into the banking modality. I have described this mechanism briefly for the Canadian scene, which differs from that of the United States. (Most countries have special twists and turns in the annihilation mechanisms of their central banks but the principle remains the same.)

It is a peculiarity of economic activity that probably follows from the high speed at which it takes place, that structures and procedures set up for dealing with relatively minor problems often end up being used for much larger problems. Almost without our noticing it is happening, those structures and procedures grow into vital roles. The mechanism whereby the Bank of Canada annihilates obligations is a clear example of this peculiarity. The first governor of the bank, Mr. Graham Towers, as Prof. Blackman has pointed out, had little to do in his first few years, in fact, for well over a decade because of the intrusion of the Second World War. Early in the 1950's, however, he put a contract in place that is of great importance. Called the "Purchase and Resale Agreement", it effectively made the Bank of Canada lender of last recourse to a group of brokers (called "designated brokers" in the agreement and "money market dealers" in the money market). Since at that time the government was not a massive deficit-financer, the only immediate need Graham Towers had for this Agreement was to smooth out very minor overdraft circumstances the government (his client) might have for short periods with the private banks. After all, if part of your job is exerting "moral suasion" on bankers, then being overdrawn, if only for a moment, makes it difficult to carry on a serious discussion with them. Whatever else he wanted, Graham Towers wanted to be taken seriously.

In this Agreement, these brokers, who undertook to "job" (i.e. be wholesalers for) Treasury Bills (T-Bills),[46] pledged to bid on all offerings of them by the bank. In return, they were able to sell T-Bills held in their portfolios to the bank under an agreement whereby they were to purchase those T-Bills back at a stated price in a short period of time, not exceeding 2½ days. Effectively, therefore, the Purchase and Resale Agreement makes it possible for the Bank of Canada to *lend to its lenders so that they can lend to it.* For many years, the "stated price" for buying back the T-Bills has been ¼ of 1% above the average price at which the last offering of T-Bills was made by the bank. Thus, the Bank of Canada sold 3-month T-Bills on November 12, 1980, in the amount of $790 million at an average yield of 12.42%. That is an annual yield so that what really happened was that money market dealers paid $100−(12.42÷4) = $ 96.89 for a government obligation due in three months for $100. In that same week, the maximum loan by the bank to the brokers under Purchase and Resale was $39 million. That loan cost them ¼ of 1% and since it probably existed for not more than two days it cost $39 million x .0025 x (2÷365) = $534.25. This was not a typical week for the current situation. Purchase and Resale loans are usually upwards of $300 million in today's scene so that the ¼ of 1% charge tends to exceed $5,000 in any given week. That charge added to the average T-Bill rate, by the way, is now the rate the Bank of Canada charges for loans to the private banks since it fixes that "Bank Rate" or "Rediscount Rate" at ¼ of 1% above the average 3-month T-Bills.[47] In other words, the private banks can rediscount their paper with the Bank of Canada at the same rate as applies to brokers under the Purchase and Resale Agreement for T-Bills.

To pursue this example a bit further, on November 12, 1980, 3-month bills *coming due* totalled $740 million so that net new borrowing on 3-month bills was $790 − $740 = $50 million of which the bank loaned something up to $39 million under Purchase and Resale. At the same time, however, the bank borrowed $320 million at 6 months term at an average rate of 12.77%, of which it needed $360 million to pay back 6-month bills falling due on that date—in short, it did not borrow enough at 6-months term to pay back what was due. It was $40 million short. But it borrowed $50 million more than it needed at 3-months term to pay out 3-month bills falling due. To do that, however, it actually had to lend up to $39 million. Clearly, that $39 million or a sum approaching it represents newly printed money which is a liability of the Bank of Canada that it owes to the Government of Canada. Since the bank lends it to the brokers, however, it is also an asset of the bank. In other words the obligation for the new money is *annihilated* in the bank's balance sheet.

The effect of the loans to brokers so that they can lend to the bank is of course to dull the sharp sensitivity of the private banks to withdrawals made by ultimate holders of the government T-Bills. As I have said previously, this allows the central bank to edge the proceeds of the bond sale into government deposits with the private banks even though the government's debt structure ratio is falling below .50, at which level they would tend to reject such deposits and seek deposits from the solvent entities that are largely the ultimate holders of government bonds.

I use the term "edge" for the following reasons. As those lenders to government buy the bonds from the brokers (usually within 48 hours of the Thursday auction), they are not in general net depositors but net withdrawers from their accounts. Before they make those withdrawals, the private banks have already made extensive loans to the brokers so that they can buy the issue of T-Bills. Thus, a loan structure has been developed involving large sums that *requires* deposits to equate it if only for the day or so until the brokers pay back their loan out of proceeds of retail sale. Otherwise, banking modality is threatened. As the draw-down of deposits of the ultimate holders of the T-Bills starts and the influx of deposits from the brokers back-fills behind them, there must be a short-fall because of the repayments brokers must make to the central bank under Purchase and Resale. (Essentially, they must buy back the T-Bills they hypothecated.) There is thus always some room for government deposits to enter the bank to support an already existing loan structure even though the chequing flow accompanying them is such that the banks can create little credit out of them.

In effect what I am saying is that under such circumstances, retaining the banking modality of a debt structure ratio near unity is *of the essence.* Government deposits, although undesirable, are needed as "cover" and hence are accepted. As a result, the government's debt structure ratio falls. It retains its private banking connections. The banks accept the newly printed money of government. By a repetition of essentially the same events week after week, the central bank can force truly substantial quantities of new money into the system even though its client's debt structure ratio falls rapidly in the range less than .50 at which the leverage of the private banks is being hurt.

The essential point is that "putting money into the economy" is not an easy thing to do for the central bank once its government is insolvent. *Massive* injections are out of the question. Both the Purchase and Resale Agreement in Canada and the rediscounting technique in the United States are insidious drip-drip processes in which it must never become evident to the banks that they are being tricked.

The meaning of the banking modality becoming the essence is of course that as this "forcing" happens, the banks make less and less on hard transactions which yield the bulk of the net worth proportion of their natural 8% reserve on payables. That is, their net worth becomes a smaller and smaller fraction of their natural reserves and their generated savings from soft transactions becomes a larger and larger proportion. This is shown to have been the case for Canada's Big 5 banks in Appendix III. The net worth share of their natural reserves fell from 44% in 1969 to 31% in 1980, as the share of their generated savings from soft transactions rose from 8% to 24%. The share of their generated savings from hard transactions, on the other hand, remained almost exactly 50% to 1979, but it fell to 45% in 1980.

Thus we are starting to see the anatomy of our slavery to inflation. Indeed, the activities of the central bank are actually *burning out* the net worth share of natural reserves of our banking system. Of course as this happens the banks carry out interacting processes of raising prime rates and then pushing dollars over the border so that the dollar falls in foreign currency. The central bank must intervene to stop the decline in the dollar because a major receivable it holds is foreign currency and if it rises significantly its own banking modality is threatened and its banking candle will be snuffed out. The obvious way for it to make this intervention is to back out of the debt market and let interest rates rise thus stopping the burn-out of the private banks. It cannot do this, however, because what is powering the system is the government's debt structure ratio, which is to say if the bank starts paying back debt rather than rolling it over plus new borrowing, before that debt structure ratio is increased sufficiently, the government's obligations (interest payments on bonds, public service wages, etc.) will not be met.

Since it cannot back out (and in fact if it could back out the bank would never have been needed in the first place), it goes forward. It has the machinery in place to allow the government to go merrily on its way, deficit-financing, and taking its debt structure ratio down and down. It passes .45 as if it did not exist. It whizzes by .40; it waves at .35. When it starts to approach .30, however, a very strange sequence of events gives it pause. If we can get our minds around this sequence of events we will be well on our way to understanding a great deal about how ALL economies work.

CHAPTER 8

The First Stage of Scientific Bankruptcy

I hope the reader will tolerate a few very simple uses of illustrations. We happen to be at a point at which with a combination of the reader's commonsense knowledge of how businesses work and a way of putting that knowledge into pictures, we can capture the sequence of events our deficit-financing government encounters as its debt structure ratio approaches .30.[48]

Everybody knows that one of the functions carried out by all economic entities is collecting the moneys owed to them. If an entity is owed a great deal of receivables and owes very few payables, collecting a particular "next" dollar of receivables is, in general, less immediately important than it is if that situation is reversed and it is owed very little, but owes a great deal.

Let us represent a dollar of receipts, i.e. collected receivables, by a straight vertical line. If it helps us, we can think of that line as a bow string. If we do that, then we can think of the *importance* of collecting that dollar as the length of the bow we string with it. To accommodate cases of lower and lower ratios of total receivables to total payables (lower and lower debt structure ratios), we make the following chart:

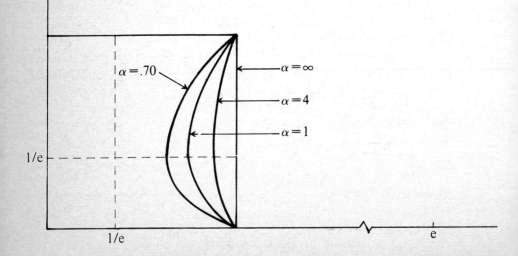

Chart I
Degrees of Importance
of Collecting $1 of Receivables

Each of these lines representing a bow we are stringing with the right hand vertical straight line is labelled α_1, α_2 and so on. The first bow is itself a straight line and it is labelled $\alpha_1 = \infty$ meaning that the debt structure ratio is extremely high. The bow marked α_2 refers to a lower ratio, α_3, one that is still lower and so on. For reasons that will emerge in a moment, I have drawn our bows a bit off-centre as if the wood in them had less resiliency in the lower half than it has in the upper half.

Each of our bows is an "arc length" which, in comparison with our bow string, measures the importance placed upon a dollar of receipts being collected.

Our common experiences tell us as well that withholding paying a dollar of payables is not very important in entities that are owed a great deal compared with what they owe. But as the debt structure ratio falls, such withholding becomes more and more important. Anyone who has run a business knows that "hold up that cheque a few days" is one of the commonest expressions used in it. Nearly every householder knows also that in running the household such practices are not uncommon and that they relate to what is coming in compared with what is going out.

We can represent these increases in the importance of not paying a dollar by the illustration (Chart II) on page 66.

I have drawn this illustration horizontally in contrast to the last which was drawn vertically. The reason for doing this will emerge in a moment.

The length of the bow that we string represents the importance of *not* paying a dollar of payables. For each of our +'s on the previous illustration, we have one on this.

Now let us put our two illustrations together. The rationale for doing this is found in an ancient aphorism we all know, namely, that

"a dollar saved is a dollar earned."

This tells us that if we do not pay out a dollar that we have it is the same thing as collecting a dollar. In both cases, we *have* a dollar, which is to say, they are alternate ways of "having" a dollar.

In putting the diagrams together, therefore, let us interpret this aphorism to mean that a dollar *not* paid equals a dollar collected in the sense of *intersection* at right angles of our two straight lines (Chart III on page 67).

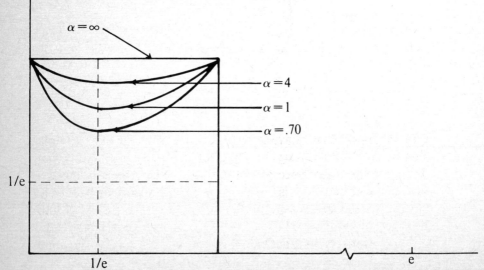

Chart II
Degrees of Importance
of Postponing Payment of $1 of Payables

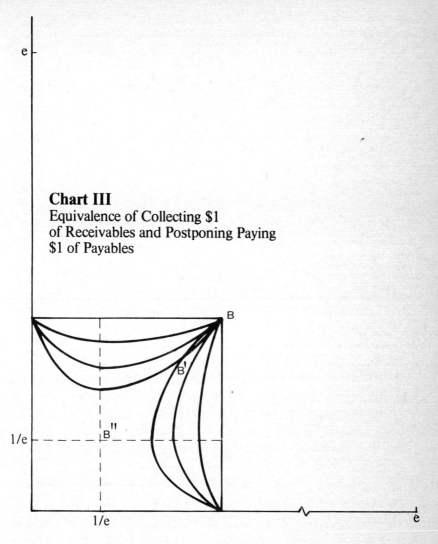

Chart III
Equivalence of Collecting $1
of Receivables and Postponing Paying
$1 of Payables

It might appear that I have been arbitrary in drawing our two dollar lengths, one representing the importance of collecting a dollar and the other the importance of not paying a dollar, at right angles to each other. In fact, that is not the case. Our debt structure ratios are quoted in succession as an infinite number of dollars of receivables *per dollar* of payables, $4 of receivables per dollar of payables and so on. If we think of each debt structure ratio as existing permanently, therefore, if that ratio is .70, for example, collecting a dollar and not paying a dollar are of equal importance, and collecting 70¢ and not paying 70¢ are of equal importance. Thus, each of our debt structure ratio arc lengths must intersect, not only at the point marked B, but also at the points such as marked by B′ and B″, and so on. All of those points must lie on a line OB at 45° to the two straight lines. In other words, AB and CB must be at right angles to each other.[49]

So much for the collection and payment postponement aspects of running a business, a government, or our own lives. The arc lengths clearly give us a type of measure of the importance of these activities as the debt structure ratio falls. There is more than this to the problems facing all of us in running our economic lives. We not only collect receivables and postpone payment; we take various actions to ensure that receiv*ables* themselves are generated and we also take action to ensure that pay*ables* are *not* generated.

Now if we have a plethora of receivables compared with our payables (a very high debt structure ratio), then generating a new receivable to compensate for one we have already collected is relatively unimportant. This is so because we still have many receivables left. Naturally, if our debt structure ratio is lower, generating new receivables becomes more important to us.

Similarly, the lower the debt structure ratio is the more important it will be not to generate payables. I propose to represent these two conditions on our diagram in the following manner— (Chart IV on page 69).

The lines AB and CB have two interpretations. The first, readers will recall, was that AB represented the importance of collecting a dollar of receivables; CB the importance of postponing the payment of a dollar of payables. When the debt structure ratio is infinitely high, the importance of those activities (collecting and postponing) is negligible. Consequently I have represented it by the shortest distance between the points A and B, and C and B. Now we find a second interpretation. The lines (let us say the right and top "edges" of them) also represent the fact that *generating* (as distinct from collecting) a dollar of receivables and postponing the generation (as distinct from the payment) of a dollar of payables is also of extremely low importance as the debt structure ratio approaches infinity.

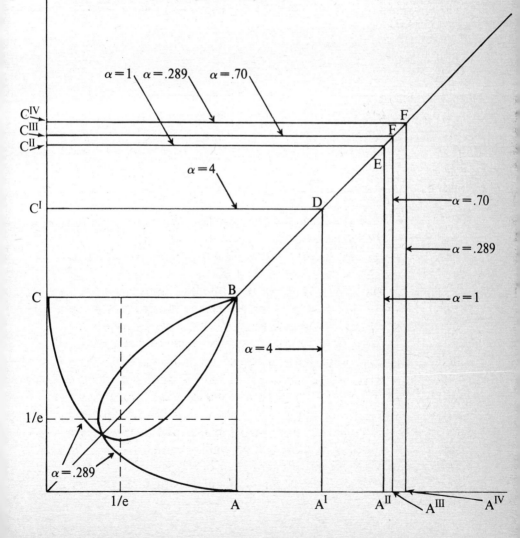

Chart IV
Comparison of Importance of Generating
$1 Receivables with Collecting $1 of Receivables
and Postponing Generating $1 of Payables
with Postponing Paying $1 of Payables

Thinking of this second representation, then, as the debt structure ratio is taken lower and lower (i.e. "down" from infinity), the lengths of the straight vertical lines $A^I D$, $A^{II} E$, $A^{III} F$, and $A^{IV} G$, represent the increasing importance of generating receivables, and the straight horizontal lines $C^I D$, $C^{II} E$, $C^{III} F$ and $C^{IV} G$, represent the increasing importance of postponing generating a dollar of payables.

We therefore have two crucial lengths for each value of the debt structure. One is the arc length representing the importance of collecting a dollar of receivables or postponing a dollar of payments. The former stretches from A to B and the latter from C to B for each debt structure ratio. The other length represents the importance of generating a dollar of receivables or postponing generating a dollar of payables. The former stretches vertically from A to B, A^I to D, A^{II} to E, etc. for each debt structure ratio whereas the latter stretches horizontally from C to B, C^I to D, C^{II} to E, etc. for each debt structure ratio.[50]

The reason I have inflicted this essay in pictorial representation on the reader is that it allows us to visualize, in terms that are not too abstract or too far away from the reader's general experience in the real world, the nature of the basic laws that underlie Objective Economics. Those laws, which are deduced from that science's two assumptions—that obligations are met, and that money per se carries no magic with it[51]—do in fact yield arc lengths and straight lines as identified in the last paragraph and *allow us to calculate their lengths in great accuracy, indeed to as many decimal points as we wish.*[52] Those calculations lead us to the discovery that at a debt structure ratio of .289, i.e. just less than .30, the length of the line representing the importance of generating a dollar of receivables (or *not* generating a dollar of payables) *becomes less than the length of the line representing the importance of the collection of a dollar of receivables or not paying a dollar of payables.* Further, as the debt structure ratio continues to fall, the amount by which the former line is shorter than the latter increases.

At the debt structure ratio of .289, therefore, the *collection* of a dollar of receivables is more important than the *generation* of that dollar of receivables. Similarly, *not* paying a dollar of payables is more important than *not* generating that dollar of payables. From the former of these circumstances we conclude that the entity's personnel are out beating the bushes to collect moneys already owed to the entity more than they are trying to generate new receivables. From the latter we conclude that the entity's personnel are struggling far harder *not* to pay a payable than they are not to generate a new payable; that is, they incur bills far easier than they pay them. I refer to those circumstances as scientific bankruptcy. They begin to exist when the debt structure ratio has fallen to .289.

In note 45, I pointed out that the distinction between a government's fiscal policy and its monetary policy (which is largely carried out by the central bank) is, in business terms, the distinction between "running the business", and "collecting receivables and postponing paying payables". What we have just discovered, therefore, is that when the government's debt structure ratio hits .289 and continues to fall as deficits continue, *the activities of the central bank are more important than the activities of the government*. Indeed, as the insolvency progresses, the government activity, i.e. what is really going on in government, *is* the activity of its central bank, and until the central bank has performed its functions of collecting receivables and postponing paying payables, *generating new payables is all that goes on in government*. This is one element of freedom left for running the business of government because we know that *not* paying a payable is now more important than not generating it. In short, it can be generated with impunity. What is more important is that it not be paid. The other freedom that is left is that of *not* generating receivables, because collecting them is more important.

Thus, as we mentioned earlier, at a debt structure ratio of .289, fiscal policy has become the creature of the central bank; the bank has enslaved the government. Our central banks are the masters since what they do has become more important than running the government. Yet, through its exercise, however dwindling, of fiscal policy, the government still has the freedoms to generate payables and not to generate receivables. In effect, therefore, incurring more and more liabilities is one of its avenues of activity, and the other is *not* generating receivables, i.e. not maintaining taxes. In fact, *lowering* taxes is its freedom on the revenue side.

When I use the term "freedom" in these senses, I hasten to add that I am referring to the type of freedom a man has to fall with acceleration if he steps out of an airplane flying at 10,000 feet. That is, it is freedom *within* natural law. In other words, at or below a debt structure ratio of .289, the government *will* increase the generation of its payables virtually in step with its withholding payment of them (i.e. rolling debt over by refunding). The government *will* decrease the generation of its tax receivables virtually in step with the increase in its collection of a dollar of taxes. If it does not actually reduce tax rates or bases or both, it will give tax money back in the form of "tax credits".

Of course it seems incredible that a deficit-financing government that has progressively brought its servant, its central bank, to the level of its slavemaster, would pursue "policies" that involve increased generation of payables and decreased generation of receivables. I emphasize two points, however, one of them taken from real life and the other from the natural science of Objective Economics. The real life point is that what I say will happen is precisely what *is* happening. Government after government is rapidly increasing the generation of payables as it sharply increases the share of its debt that is "paid back", by simply rolling it over into new debt. That is, it is withholding the payment of payables to an increasing extent as it generates them with acceleration. On the side of not generating receivables, on the other hand, government after government is in the throes of escalating tax credit schemes, and one government, that in the USA, has just been elected on a pledge to cut taxes. The fact it was elected pledged also to cut expenditure is true but its top priority and, in my view as dictated by Objective Economics, all it will be able to do, is cut taxes. Nature will not allow it to cut expenditures unless it can either sell off enough assets to raise its debt structure ratio substantially above .289, or unless it steals, which is to say, expropriates to levels hitherto unimagined. The rise of interest rates and/or fall of the dollar caused by its insolvency will ensure that its expenditures do not fall and in fact do rise.[53]

The second point is that the reason we find these modalities incredible is that we think the economy and the government's part of it are domains with which and over which man has control. We know from Chapter 2 that that is not true. Nature's laws are in control and those laws force two facts upon us. One is that obligations are always met if only by the creditor. That one is easy to grasp. The second law is that, try as we might, we cannot take away from a dollar of money its essential property: when it is discounted, whether the discounting is real or implied, that discounting is exactly equated, and hence obliterated, by its accumulation. This law is not easy to grasp. It is, however, the working of these two laws that created central banks to accommodate governmental deficits when the private banks would have stopped them. It is the working of these two laws that elevated those creatures of governmental insolvency to the level of slave-masters. It is the working of these laws that left government, the slave, "free" to commit the most senseless acts, such as generating even more payables and less receivables. Thus we find the Ministers of the Federal Government of Canada running around creating payables of unheard-of magnitude, payables on which the Bank of Canada will withhold payment virtually to the end of time. At the same time they are falling all over themselves to give taxes back, and to avoid generating receivables, while the government's cash requirements are so high that the largest single buyer of its own bonds is the Bank of Canada.

Are we finished with the slavery story? Does nature decree that an insolvent government that purports to represent the free spirit of the people ends up the slave of its central bank? No, we are not finished. There is a final stage, a stage that I call "break-up", at which two new alternative slaveries occur. One is the slavery to theft or expropriation. The other is the slavery to sell-off of government assets, i.e. "privatization". A major thesis of this book is that society must resist government, even though governments are not to blame for the inflation they have caused. It must stop governments from resorting to theft; it must force them into privatization. After we have told the story of these ultimate conditions forced on government by nature's laws, we shall have the full catalogue of man's slavery to inflation written.

CHAPTER 9

Bankruptcy—The Ultimate Condition

Much earlier in Part II I said we would reserve our comments upon whether or not money-issuing governments are subject to the same rules, i.e. natural economic laws, as other entities. Is there, in short, something about the magic of money or money-issuing powers that allows government to do what non-government cannot, namely, adopt and adhere to, virtually forever, a modality of deficit financing?

The answer clearly is no. Money and money-issuing powers hold no magic. They do, however, hold great complexity. It is because we have not understood that complexity, that is, that Keynes, Friedman, etc.—an economic profession of subjectivism—did not understand that complexity, that modern society fell into the tragedy of modern inflation. It is in the mistaken egocentrism with which that profession views the economy that we have failed to interpret the facts around us. They are facts that have created central banks; facts that have reduced central bankers to all the dizzying second-by-second activity of acting out the role of bankrupts concealing their bankruptcy. They are facts that have reduced some of the finest public services in the world (such as that of Canada) to jellies quivering with "inefficiency" as they wait for the central bank to perform its bankruptcy functions of collecting receivables and postponing payment of payables. They are facts which have taken rates of interest to spectacular highs in perturbation with exchange rates of spectacular lows; facts that have left totally unshielded the rapid increase of government payables and have similarly freed government from regeneration and increase of its receivables. They are facts that our common experiences tell us can lead to only one end: the break-up of government itself.

Our common experiences tell us that when the roll-over portion of new borrowing approaches 100%, the game is in its ninth innings; that when the central bank is the largest single lender to government, the final curtain is falling; and that when the time term of the paper we sell to borrow becomes shorter and shorter, and long term borrowing ceases to have any meaning, the car that just entered the parking lot is that of the local bailiff. Since we know all this, it is somewhat of an anti-climax to pursue Objective Economics to its final implication of deficit financing, namely, break-up of the entity. We do so, not to demonstrate nature's laws that compel the entity to break up, but to demonstrate that even in that break-up nature is so beneficent that it still leaves us a choice. The whole question of whether mankind's freedom will survive rests upon how that choice is made.

The following extension of our last chart, which we can make in our imagination, shows us what break-up is scientifically and the debt structure ratio at which it happens. When the debt structure ratio has fallen to below $.135 = 1/e^2$, the two arc lengths that represent the importance of collecting a dollar of receivables and postponing the payment of a dollar of payables acquire another pair of intersections. Previously we pointed out that when the debt structure ratio was .70, collecting 70¢ was the same as *not* paying 70¢, and when that ratio was .60, collecting 60¢ was the same as *not* paying 60¢. Now we find that if that ratio is .10, i.e. less than .135, then collecting 10¢ is the same as not paying 10¢, *but* collecting 12¢ is the same as not paying 8¢ *and* collecting 8¢ is the same as *not* paying 12¢. As the debt structure ratio falls, the spread between 8¢ and 12¢ for these new intersections widens. How are we to interpret these facts in real life terms?[54]

Again, our common experiences guide us. We are all familiar with those unhappy circumstances in which the creditors and debtors of an entity meet and an agreement is reached in which "66.6¢ on the dollar" is the resolution of the financial problems for the entity. That is the case implied for a debt structure ratio of .10 mentioned in the previous paragraph because $^8/_{12}$ = .666.

Now the expression "66.6¢ on the dollar" can be interpreted in two ways. One way implies that people who are *owed* $1.00 will in fact *receive* 66.6¢ in payment of it. The other way implies that for every 66.6¢ the entity is owed, it will *take* $1.00. In normal business practice, it is the former that applies, i.e. the entity pays out payables at less than their face. Indeed, bankruptcy laws are extremely specific about how this will be done if parties to the transaction are to stay out of jail. When we are talking about government, however, at least in countries with laws such as those of England or Canada, in which the supremacy of the judiciary is not at all clear, the bankruptcy laws are assumed not to apply. This opens the way for the second meaning of "66.6¢ on the dollar", which is to say, it is possible that the bankrupt government will simply take away from others more than it is owed. "Expropriation" is the term used for this.

There is of course the third alternative of the intersection at 10¢ itself. This really is not an alternative, however, because all economic activity, i.e. incurring obligations and meeting them, involves tiny bits of what is called "float". For example, when we deposit cash in the bank in an interest-bearing savings account, our account does not start to earn interest for a few hours or even a few days. Similarly, when we borrow money at interest, we usually do not start paying interest for a few days. The existence of float always implies very slight movements in the direction of either receiving more than we give, or receiving less than we give. In short, reality is always $1.00001 for $1.00000 or $.99999 for $1.00. Those slight movements or perturbations are dampened out for debt structure ratios down to .135. Below that ratio, however, they tend to augment until the new intersections are met, i.e. 8¢ for 12¢, etc. In effect, therefore, there is no third alternative in the real world and the entity with a debt structure ratio below .135 either expropriates, which is to say steals, or it goes the opposite route of "settling accounts".

Although there is no third alternative, settling accounts in this manner need not mean or imply the disappearance of the entity. As long as generating the next dollar of receivables after the one being generated now is more important than collecting the one being generated now, and as long as postponing generating the next dollar of payables after the one being generated now is more important than postponing payment of the one being generated now, there is still the possibility of selling off assets to obtain receivables and thus getting rid of payables and still operating the entity with what is left. This "ultimate" circumstance is reached when the debt structure ratio has fallen to between .07 and .08. Thus, there remains some running room between a ratio of $.135 = 1/e^2$ and .08 in which *privatization* can still save the ship.

For the moment we still have two matters to tidy up. One is the statement of what inflation is as seen in the perspectives of Objective Economics. The other is to put together, in a single piece, our vision of the nature of our slavery to inflation. Part III is devoted to these matters.

PART III

THE NATURE OF OUR SLAVERY TO INFLATION

CHAPTER 10

Inflation and Depreciation of the Currency

Before we pick our way back through Parts I and II and try to find the specific sense or senses in which mankind is in slavery to inflation, we must be sure that we understand what inflation is. In the discoveries of Objective Economics we find that we cannot accept that chestnut of modern "wisdom" that inflation is "too much money chasing too few goods". In its place, what do we accept?

Objective Economics leads us not to a concept of *relative* value, i.e. *one* thing being worth so much of *another* thing. It leads us to a concept of *absolute* value, the viewpoint that dominated the economic thought of the Middle Ages and that recurred in part at least in the value thought form of the classical authors of the late 18th and early 19th centuries, Quesnay, Smith, Malthus, and Ricardo. It was also the turn of mind of Karl Marx.

In the value concept of Objective Economics we say, in distinction from inflation is "too much money chasing too few goods", that inflation is a *depreciation of the currency*. The most familiar evidence of inflation that is nearly always with us is individual entities entering into insolvency and in so doing, "settling accounts" at, for example, 60¢ on the dollar.

In the next few pages I hope to convince you that that statement that inflation is a depreciation of the currency does not imply the other and indeed it is because professionals and non-professionals have not been able to raise their sights above the other that we have not understood what inflation is and have therefore not understood our slavery to it.

Perhaps understandably, in examining the question of valuation, economic literature headed straight for what seemed to be the obvious main problem, and turned its back on a rather less obvious one. The literature concerned itself almost exclusively with the valuation of items that were frequently exchanged *by* entities, items that perhaps conceivably could be organized into various "quantities" of "units", and largely ignored the valuation of *the entities themselves*. The problem of *how entities are themselves valued*, therefore, is either not faced at all in that literature or, when it is, it is treated as a subject almost outside the purview of the economist.

Let us pursue this through two kinds of activity. If a car manufacturer, for example, could produce cars without using any equipment, without using any buildings, without any unfinished stages of production and with zero profit, so that his cars were virtually "born" by an immaculate conception as it were, then clearly the *value* of his company would be the total value of the cars it had produced and not sold. Thus, if we could *value* his company we would by the same ability have valued his cars! Of course, virtually none of those conditions holds for a car manufacturer. Equipment and buildings are required; residues are left ranging from unused supplies through scrap and near scrap; cars exist in various stages of completion; and a profit (or loss) residue results. These real facts have weighed heavily in the balance with economists and have undoubtedly made their literature shy away from tackling the valuation problem of the entity as distinct from the valuation problem of cars. Essentially, orientation to the cars has led to a "demand and supply economics" in which value is seen as the "price" that equates the two at a certain volume of sale. Price of course is a quantity of one thing given for another and since we usually quote it in the currency unit (rather than the car unit) we are led to seeing inflation as too much of the currency (money) chasing too few cars (goods). Thus to get rid of inflation we say we must either *decrease* the amount of money or *increase* the quantity of cars.

But let us consider banks, which are a different type of entity. We know that banks do not "produce" loans, because they borrow loans back in the act of making them. Thus the production act for loans is nullified. We know also that they do not "produce" deposits because when they borrow they immediately lend what they borrow or they annihilate the obligation. They do, however, *produce* money and they do not cancel out the act by taking money back. Banks cash our cheques and it is only after a roundabout process of circulation that they get that money back.

Further, in their money-producing activity, banks undergo virtually zero accumulated depreciation as a proportion of their total payables and receivables.[55] In addition, once they come up with money and put it in your hands and mine, we spend it and it gets back to the bank, not worn out and reprocessed the way a car is when it gets back to a car manufacturer as steel forms, but more or less in good shape. Thus, although at any given time all the currency is divided into perhaps 1/5th in the hands of the banks and 4/5ths in the hands of the general public, over any significant period all of it may be said to pass through the hands of banks in its original form. It is in fact as if all non-bank holders of the currency were parking lots for the banks' currency.

It follows from the fact that banks are, as stated above, *producers* of money and that that is essentially all they produce, and from the fact that all currency keeps on going through their hands so that in a sense they always "have" it no matter where it is "parked", that if we knew the laws determining how all banks have been valued theoretically, we would know how all currency was valued, theoretically. The value of banks would simply be the value of the currency. By comparing that value, let's call it the "natural value" of banks, with the *market price* of all banks in the stock market, we would be able to say whether the banks and hence the currency had *ap*preciated or *de*preciated relative to their natural value. Thus, if the stock market price of the banks were higher than their natural price, then that would mean that the currency they produce had appreciated by that difference. If that difference were $200 million, for example, and $10 billion currency existed, the appreciation would be 2%, which is to say, each $1 would be worth $1.02. On the other hand, if the stock market price of all banks were less than the natural value of the banks by $200 million for the same amount of currency, the *de*preciation would be 2%, which is to say $1 would be worth $.98.

This concept of depreciation and appreciation of the currency obviously introduces two concepts of value. One is what the stock market tells us banks *are* worth as a total (which we can discover by multiplying the price of bank shares by the number of shares issued). The other is a "natural" price concept that tells us what the banks *should* be worth, given their economic state. If we have demonstrated that natural price *should be* the price the stock market price *tends to become*, the fact it has not done so to a precise degree represents and measures appreciation or depreciation of the currency and hence deflation and inflation. Further, deflation or inflation measured in such a manner are evidently the product of some type of economic work that is hindering adjustments that should take place.

This approach is to be compared with one in which we say that the measure of inflation is the percentage change upwards in an average of prices such as the Consumer Price Index. Such a measure simply tells us that that average has increased, a fact most consumers already suspect. Our approach, by contrast, compares an actual price that *exists* now, with a price that *should* exist now, if the natural price obtained. If the actual price is lower than the natural price, then we can calculate the amount of the depreciation of the currency. With absolutely no reference to "goods", therefore, or "money chasing goods", we measure the depreciation of the currency.

The questions of course are: what is the natural price of entities in general, including banks; and is there evidence that market prices of entities do approach their natural prices?

CHAPTER 11

Natural Value

The British economist David Ricardo (circa 1820) took the view that the currency had a natural price. That natural price was seen by Ricardo as the cost of production of the currency. The difference between Ricardo's view and mine is that he meant the cost of production of precious metals which in his day circulated as currency, whereas I mean the cost of production of currency as measured by the natural value of banks. That natural value in turn is a special case of the natural value of all entities.

Consider a case in which you and I are buying a well established bank. We would first obtain its balance sheet, indeed a number of successive balance sheets. Our eyes would quickly travel down the right hand sides of those sheets (left hand in Britain) and settle on the number called "equity" or "net worth". Since that number represents the best efforts of the accounting profession to tell us (and the bank) what the bank is "worth", its discovery would undoubtedly "scale" our problem for us.

Now net worth is basically the original funds put into the bank by its owners to which have been added profits that have not been distributed and new equity funds that may have been raised in the equity market for new offerings of shares. In itself, net worth makes no allowance for the fact that the bank is well established with a large body of depositors and borrowers. Also, in itself, net worth makes no allowance for an essential quality we have mentioned before, namely that to *be* a bank it must have sufficient foreign banking contacts so that obligations it enters into by its deposits can be quickly annihilated in soft transactions if hard transactions happen not to be readily available. Thus, net worth (N), falls short of "valuing" the bank on two counts. First of all, it makes no allowance for the establishment of a continuing mechanism for transforming deposits into loans, loans into deposits. A major part of this "asset" is the ability of the bank to raise its rates on existing demand loans. Secondly, it makes no allowance for the mechanism that has been established for annihilating obligations. This second omission is of course unique to the credit-generating entities in the economy, of which the banking system is the major part. The activities involved in establishing an on-going business, however, will have to be considered in valuing virtually any company, bank or not, that we might think of buying.

One purpose of the stock market study was to test a very specific hypothesis about the manner in which the stock market values companies. The hypothesis was that the total market price of the listed companies tends to fluctuate around, and hence approach, the sum of two quantities: net worth (N), and what I have called "generated savings" (E_t). Both quantities are aggregated for all companies in the aggregate.

This test was remarkably successful.[56]

Since it works, and since the generated savings resulting from the mechanism of annihilating obligations is a relatively small number of dollars compared with E_t and N,[57] there is strong evidence that the law stated above is the *objective law of valuation* which tells us the natural value that all entities, including banks, tend to approach.

Given this proof that our law of objective valuation works, inflation reveals itself in our data by a remarkably persistent and rapidly increasing divergence of the value the market places upon banks below their natural value. In actual fact, looking to the Canadian scene, when we aggregate all entities that create credit and have consistent near-unity debt structure ratios (about 75% of the total being the Big 5 banks) we find that whereas market price fell short of their natural value by $457 million in 1969, the shortfall was $9.140 billion in January 1979, and I estimate it to be $11.882 billion in January 1981. Since that shortfall spreads over the total currency issue, we obtain the following table of natural values for the currency for the period 1969 to 1981:

	(1)	(2)	(3)
	Amount of Inflation = Shortfall	Currency Issue	$1 − (1)/(2)
Year	(Natural Value of Banks* − Stock Market Value of Banks)	(Bank of Canada Monthly Revue)	(Natural Value of the Currency)[58]
	(10^6)	(10^6)	($1)
1969	457	3,446	.867
1970	1,128	3,632	.689
1971	887	4,103	.784
1972	349	4,806	.927
1973	720	5,551	.870
1974	3,994	6,290	.365
1975	3,768	7,283	.483
1976	5,406	7,813	.308
1977	6,992	8,638	.191
1978	8,234	9,539	.137
1979	9,140	10,314	.113
1980 (Jan.81)	11,882	11,108	−.069

*Net worth plus generated savings from hard and soft transactions of the banks.

Thus starting 11 years ago when the natural value of the Canadian dollar was already more than 13¢ less than a dollar, it fell even further in 1970, rose in 1971 and 1972 to a high of almost 93¢, fell in 1973 slightly, but in 1974, the year of the sharp drop in the stock market, it fell rapidly to 36½¢. It regained a bit of value in 1975 (the year in which wage and profit controls were imposed) but since then it has fallen sharply. In fact, as of my estimates for January 1981, the natural value of the Canadian dollar is *less than zero* by almost 7¢!

One way to obtain some grasp of what is involved here is to visualize a coin that is made by a royal counterfeiter such as Henry VIII with a base metal core. As we go from its core to its outside coating, the metal becomes rarer and rarer until finally it is gold. Such a coin, when it is newly minted, can be assumed to be a fraudulent promise to pay a stated weight of the outside metal. As the coin is used, the outer metal is clipped off by the king each time it is returned to him and it is now a silver coin, next a copper coin, then an iron coin and so on. When all the gold is clipped away there is *no* currency issue in terms of the gold unit of currency referred to in column 3 of the above table. In a sense, therefore, the number from column 2 is zero minus infinity. When all the silver is clipped away then there is no currency issue in terms of the silver unit of currency. Again, therefore, the natural value of the silver currency is minus infinity and so on.

Relating this example to modern times we think of a dollar bill as a promise to pay a dollar bill. As the debt structure ratio of government falls each dollar bill it has succeeded in getting into the circulatory system is promised first to one person who has accepted a dollar, then to more than one but less than two. When each dollar bill is promised to exactly two people who have accepted dollar bills, then the currency has an absolute value of zero. When each dollar bill has been promised to more than two people but less than three its absolute value will be between 0 and −$1 and so on.

This default or multiple promising of the same thing manifests itself in the stock market. That is where inflation, if inflation as it is defined in Objective Economics exists, manifests itself for it is there that we can buy a dollar for less than a dollar. Specifically, stock market valuations for banks (shares issued times price) fall behind the natural value of banks. When they have fallen behind by the amount of the issued currency, the absolute value of that currency is zero.

In the language of Objective Economics, the natural value of banks is an objective promise to the banks to pay that value for the banks. It is like receivables. The actual market price of the banks is, on the other hand, like payables and is an objective promise to the non-banks to pay that amount to them. The ratio of natural to actual value is called the "ownership structure ratio." The TSE study established that just as debt structure ratios tend to a narrow central range of values, ownership structure ratios do so as well to the same narrow range. Thus, we have strong evidence that the economy *does not distinguish between debt and ownership equity*. Net worth and generated savings, which are the components of natural value, which is in turn the numerator of the ownership structure ratio, tend to be paid out to owners to the same degree and in the same manner as receivables. This discovery is another return Objective Economics makes to the early classical literature. To those writers, capital was capital and return to capital tended to be seen indifferently as interest or profit on it. Our discoveries confirm their intuition.

This discussion is of necessity convoluted because the complexity of the technical argument we are skirting is very great. In actual fact the negative absolute value of the currency is associated with the penetration by the currency-issuing government of the Lee-Whiting Conditions referred to previously (note 54). In terms of those conditions we can also gain a commonsense understanding of what is involved. Imagine an economy in which all of the individuals including ourselves are so dishonest that, as every exchange happens, both parties to the exchange secretly reach into each other's pockets and take out an extra 7¢ for every dollar exchanged. Every time individuals close their books, therefore, they find they have just less than 7¢ less money than they thought they had. They have the 7¢ they stole but they did not realize 7¢ was stolen from them every time a dollar exchanged. Their balance sheet, therefore, will have to contain a write-off of about 7% and, since balance sheets must balance, that write-off, just like customers' acceptances or letters of credit in the books of banks, must appear on both sides of the books. If we extend such a situation over much time, and assume that the 7% becomes 8%, 9%, and so on, the sum of all the write-offs as a ratio of total assets = total liabilities rises higher and higher, finally consuming the whole balance sheet. This situation gives us some insight to what a negative value of the currency means. It is as if one individual settles his debts with 93¢ dollars to other individuals who settle theirs with 93¢ dollars and so on so that when we arrive back at the first individual his receivables are also being settled with 93¢ dollars which means that he now settles his debts with less than 93¢ dollars and so on.

The main thrust of this discussion, however, is not the allegation that Canada's currency has a negative absolute value and that the currency-issuing government is therefore breaking up or expropriating as the Lee-Whiting Conditions indicate. It is that the *amount of inflation is a quantity we can discover that is totally independent of the amount of the currency issue.* Changes in the amount of the currency issue or its denomination affect the natural value of the currency. They do not affect the amount of inflation. No matter what the denomination of the currency and hence its quantity in 1980, the previous table tells us that the amount of inflation in Canada was $11.882 billion in that year as compared with $9.140 billion in the previous year. In fact, taking 1969 as the base year, we claim the natural "inflation index" is as follows:

Natural Inflation Index

1969	100
1970	246
1971	194
1972	76
1973	157
1974	874
1975	824
1976	1183
1977	1530
1978	1801
1979	2000
1980	2600

This index tells us that inflation really began with a vengeance in 1970, but receded until 1974, the year of a major stock market collapse. That year saw the highest jump in inflation of any of the years included, i.e. by 550% over 1973. It decreased slightly in 1975, but it increased by 43% in 1976 over 1975, by 30% in 1977 over 1976, by 18% in 1978 over 1977, by 11% in 1979 over 1978, but by 30% in 1980 over 1979. Obviously these facts are a totally different recounting of the course of inflation than is currently used. Focussing on the irrelevancy of the course of price rise, the conventional recounting runs in terms of 5%, 8%, 10%, 12%, or whatever price rise per year, giving the impression that whatever is happening, it is not violent but to the contrary it is a rather steady, if accelerating, progression. Searching our memory for precedents, therefore, we see no similarity between what is happening today and what happened in Germany in the 1920's when the price of meals in restaurants doubled or tripled as the meals were being eaten. The fact is, however, our objective measure reveals that violent changes *are* taking place. Because the German banks had no place to go in the 1920's to annihilate obligations (the German mark was virtually unacceptable outside Germany), the whole impact of inflation fell internally to Germany and exchange price became the mode, almost the exclusive mode, of its manifestation. In short, today's inflation is internationalized, but, when conceived objectively and scientifically, we find that it is not necessarily less severe than that of Germany in the 1920's. We shall return to that startling fact in Chapter 13 in which we trace back through our various discussions and identify the nature of our slavery to inflation.

The severity of our inflation manifests itself largely in terms of the enormity of the merger activity going on. Mergers are the natural consequence of being able to buy a dollar in the stock market at different prices.

CHAPTER 12

Piety and Hope

From early in Chapter 11 it should have been evident to the reader
that man in the economy has been, is, and always will be an economic slave in one profound sense. He is a slave to natural economic
law. The fact we have failed until recently to discover that fact and
discover some of those laws has not made him less of a slave but
rather more, because he has been bound both by those laws and by
his ignorance of them.

Instead of knowledge of natural economic law freeing man to
engineer his life as his knowledge of natural physical law has freed
him, his ignorance as represented by the consensus of economic
thinkers has bound him. He and the institutions around him have
been bound by the insolvency of government, an insolvency that has
followed directly from the failure of those thinkers to grasp that insolvency has a nature. The individual, the private banks, the central
banks and their governmental clients have all suffered under the lash
of that insolvency. Springing from the soil of repetitive deficit financing, that insolvency has crushed all before it, first enslaving private
banks to subversion of their discipline by central banks, then enslaving the fiscal embodiment of our freedoms to monetary necessities,
and finally leading government itself to break-up either of itself

through privatization, or of its imaginary counter-entity components, which is to say, non-government, through the theft of expropriation. So much for the hard-won victories of representative government.

Our conventional wisdom shouts at us from every side to "balance the budget" of government. In the light of the discussion of this chapter, we have serious reasons to question the possibility of achieving this end to the succession of deficits and even more serious reasons for questioning the possibility of returning to surplus financing. First of all, we recognize that governments are part of natural economic law in the same way as you, I or US Steel. But our experiences tell us that certain situations arise in the economy that cannot be reversed. Even the largest "go belly-up" sometimes. Are we really sure that some modern governments such as the federal governments of Canada and the United States are not in that condition? Are we sure their break-up is not inevitable or so close to being inevitable that almost any major initiative will push them over the brink? Secondly, I can hardly remember the day when "balance the budget" was not a major rallying cry (and I am 58 years old). If it was ever possible, it certainly is much more difficult, if not impossible, now. Perhaps this excessive difficulty is why the last two presidents of the United States have virtually invoked the aid of God in their stern attempts to achieve the apparently unachievable.

More important than either of these considerations, however, is the fact *we* now know, that is, the readers of this book, that the deficiencies in our understanding of how economies work have been monumental. We have missed the law of constrained fall to states of least economic energy which tells us that it has not been easy for our central banks to generate enough inflation to allow economies to tolerate governmental insolvency. Indeed it has been very difficult and it is currently almost beyond the power of those institutions. We have misunderstood what limits credit expansion by the banks and failed to comprehend their *natural* reserves. Following from those failures is a basic misunderstanding of the relation between interest rates and currency exchange rates and our lack of perception of the burn-out of the private banks. We have also not grasped the objective law of valuation, which prevented us from understanding inflation itself. Inflation, it bears repeating, is a phenomenon of *absolute* depreciation of the currency (as we have seen) and *absolute* appreciation of nearly everything *but* the currency.

By seeing these two absolute phenomena as a simple ratio, which is to say, by conceiving value as relative value, subjective economists and the governments they advise missed seeing inflation itself in its relevant terms. The direct result of this has been the two equally irrelevant cries of "reduce the money supply" and/or "increase the supply of goods." Neither is the issue. The issue is the insolvency of government. Government maintains its insolvency by an absolute depreciation of what its central bank produces, namely currency, and an absolute appreciation of what it does not produce, namely everything else.

The question we must ask ourselves is: "Do these gaps in our understanding imply that there has been created world-wide a runaway self-sustaining situation we can no longer control?" Clearly we never *have* controlled it because we have never understood what we were doing. The crucial question, however, is: "Now that we do have at least the beginnings of a demonstrably relevant science that allows us to understand inflation scientifically, can we control it?" Can we, using the new science, lead governments back out of insolvency in either its low α sense (Canada, United States, Britain, etc.) or its high α sense (OPEC, Mexico, Alberta, etc.) and arrest inflation? Can we avoid the break-up of governments through their theft from each other and from non-government entities, and guide them out of the economy via a route that keeps them powerful where they must be powerful?

I emphasize that I am not certain of the answer to that last question. The concept and logical possibility of man so abusing natural laws that he might create an uncontrollable and irreversible situation threatening his very survival is very new. As a methodological and logical problem, it dates from Hiroshima. Although Einstein, Oppenheimer, and others expressed great concern about it, and partly formulated it, and although the Three Mile Island accident reminds us of it, the logic of the position is far from developed and the problem remains unsolved. We simply do not know if man can create what he cannot control.

Perhaps this is where faith must intrude. Economies have survived major insolvencies many times in history. Frequently those survivals have been accompanied by social upheavals that we now look back on as major steps forward. The War of the Spanish Succession, for example, which bankrupted the government of Louis XIV in his twilight years, clearly had much to do with creating the context for the American and French Revolutions and deepened the Industrial Revolution, all of which are viewed by most as Good Things in history. We may well ask of ourselves and of our faith, whether life would have any meaning if our present desperate slavery to inflation cannot be broken, so that man can step forward to a better future? I hope it can be done. If I did not, the last chapters of this book, which outline my plan for survival, would not have been written.

For the moment I wish to present my vision of where we are and where we shall go if we do not stop ourselves in time.

CHAPTER 13

The Burn-Out of the Economy

We recall that the natural value a non-bank entity tends to have as indicated by the stock market is the sum of its net worth (N) and its generated savings (E_t). For banks, on the other hand, their natural value is their net worth (N) plus their generated savings from hard transactions (E_t) plus their generated savings from soft transactions which I symbolize by ($\overline{E_t}$) to remind us of the annihilation mechanism such transactions involve. Central banks have a natural value that also includes these three items but additions to their net worth are ordinarily handed over to government and hence do not appear as net worth in the central banks' books. As we know from the last section, the natural value of banks is diverging more and more from their stock market value and that divergence is in fact the measure of inflation and the absolute decline in the value of the currency.

From these natural values are derived two ratios that are extremely important. For non-bank entities, the ratio is net worth divided by net worth plus generated savings, i.e. $N \div (N + E_t)$. For banks, it is net worth divided by net worth plus the banks' two kinds of generated savings, i.e. $N \div [N + E_t + (\overline{E_t})]$.

I call these "burn-out" ratios.

The outstanding fact of today's economy as represented by the

Canadian scene, which certainly is not atypical, is that the net worth of our banks is falling rapidly as a ratio with their natural value. In short, there is a steady, and sometimes sharp, switch of natural value of the banks away from net worth (as a proportion) into generated savings from hard transactions (E_t) and those from soft transactions (E_t). There is also developing a switch from the proportion of the natural value yielded by the generated savings of hard transactions into the generated savings of soft transactions. As pointed out earlier, the net worth of Canada's Big 5 banks was 44% of their natural value in 1969 whereas in 1980 it had fallen to 31%. Generated savings from soft transactions, which was only 8% of their natural value in 1969, had risen to 24% by 1980. Generated savings from hard transactions, which remained between 48% and 52% of the banks' natural value from 1969 to 1979, fell in 1980 to only 45%, giving the proportion coming from soft transactions a fillip upwards.

In fact, if we project the trends these phenomena suggest, we find that by the year 2005 the Big 5 will have less than 1% of their natural value in net worth and that value will be more or less equally split between generated savings from hard and from soft transactions. This I conceive as complete burn-out of those banks, a circumstance that I suggest cannot even be approached without collapse of one or more, and perhaps all, of them.

Collapse of the banks, however, is not the issue nearly as much as *why* it happens. It happens as the natural value of banks comes more and more to be composed of generated savings as distinct from net worth, and of generated savings from soft as distinct from hard transactions. What happens as these phenomena occur is a vast increase in trading or monetization.[59] That increase represents the *inability of the banks to wait.* They are unable to do so because of the interaction, previously discussed, between increases in the interest rate on hard transactions and soft transactions that lower exchange values of the currency. When the interest rate rises, bank net worths tend to rise more rapidly than generated savings from soft transactions. When generated savings from soft transactions rise and currency exchange values fall, however, the reverse tends to happen. But the banks are driven into soft transactions by the pressure of deposits from deficit-financing governments, deposits the banks do not want. As they have to annihilate the deposits, the number of transactions, i.e. the exchange of money for paper, paper for paper etc., that is implied by the natural value of banks, rises very quickly. This is so because one hard transaction loan and repayment adds to net worth, and hence natural value, whereas a given soft transaction, to be found, might require 10 transfers of a deposit denominated in US dollars, for example, into 10 different banks in 10 different countries. Even then the search for a customer acceptance might fail and the particular deposit will join the Eurocurrency pool, not joining in a hard transaction until some time in the future. Similarly, increases in the rate of interest on existing demand loans will imply more transactions.

Inevitably this leads to great complexity. As the banks' dependence upon soft transactions, or upon increasing rates of existing loans, rises, the rapid rise in the number of transactions causes greater and greater complexity of the things that must happen if the economy is to "work". The precise programming of events, all of which must flow smoothly into each other, grows more and more critical. Further, the scope of the damage done if some part of the program fails becomes greater. The reason this is so is that trading hangs over every part of the complex, ready to go to work with a vengeance the moment an opportunity for trading occurs. For the banks to find themselves threatened more and more every day with major catastrophes if their affairs do not work out with more and more precision is astoundingly serious. It means that they are less and less able to tolerate the affairs of their customers not working out precisely as planned. This is the situation that has created the Rolls Royce, Lockheed, Chrysler, Massey Ferguson, etc., insolvencies.

These major insolvencies never would have happened had the banking system as a whole not been so vastly involved in a type of activity requiring more and more split second precision every day of the week including week-ends. The banks have been forced into that activity by the mounting deficits of governments. Driven into soft transactions and/or rapid changes in prime rates, the multiplication of banks' transactions has been enormous. They therefore cannot wait while Massey works out its problems, while Chrysler decides what business it is in, while Lockheed decides what generation of aircraft to build, or while Rolls Royce decides who owns it.

The banks have enough problems and they cannot absorb these others.[60]

It is naive to think, as many do, that the resourcefulness of the computer will save us from any disaster that would follow from too sharp a need for split second timing. The fact is, it cannot. There is a sharply defined limit, a quantitative limit, to the amount of information any electromagnetic system can transmit without garbling the message. That limit was discovered in what is called, in electrical engineering, Shannon's Law, a law that applies as much to our brain process as to our computers. The whole economy is, in a sense, a communication system. As continuing government deficits drive the bankers to more and more multiplication of their transactions, so must the banks reserve, for their own transactions and for annihilating obligations, the capacity to make errors and correct them. So, therefore, must their capacity to absorb the errors of their customers, and to wait for them to be corrected, diminish.

This is the essence of man's slavery to inflation.[61] We can become angry at the birth of central banks to accommodate governments that must subvert banking disciplines to retain fiscal policies they identify with freedom and justice. We can become angry at central banks that finally dominate fiscal policy with their monetary exigencies. We can become angry at central governments that finally resort to theft to meet their obligations. Angry or not, however, the real issue we must face is that those of us who have not been able (and have not wished) to subvert the banking discipline find that nature's noblest creation, namely, the banking system, is forced by government deficits to be more and more unable to satisfy our needs. We started our business lives as men and women and as such we expected to make mistakes. We thought we lived in an imperfect world whose laws of nature were both beautiful and beneficent; we could make mistakes and not suffer forever because of them. Now, after more than a decade of deficit financing by government, we find we must be not men and women but gods, because the system has lost the competence to deal with our mistakes and allow us to live.

This is the slavery we face. To me, it is terrifying. So much of what we treasure in our past has been the result of trial and error, patience, plodding, stubbornness, even blind faith. Now we find ourselves in a world in which on this very day, March 8, 1981, a Sunday, a significant part of Toronto's business community is still trying to digest the Bank of Canada's $800 million or so borrowing of Thursday last and planning tomorrow, Tuesday, and Wednesday, in the hope that the Bank's "offering" of next Thursday will not catch them hopelessly in an inventory of paper that will destroy them. This is not a world that either can or will develop the world's energy resources. This is not a world that can take a problem home to a study or a garret and devote a life to its resolution. This is a world that has allowed itself to become dominated by an information flow that never needed to exist. It is a world in which a loss to a bank of a few hundred millions of dollars that in another type of world would have been quickly recuperable, is in fact equated with a loss of employment to 15,000 people that is not recuperable and creates a generation of welfare recipients whose half-life of decay can extend over many generations.

Don't blame the banks. Don't blame the people, least of all yourself. Don't even blame the central banks and their government clients. If any group is to blame it is the subjective economists, for the whole notion that deficit financing is tenable originates in their misguided discipline. Blaming them, however, is beside the point. They are as bewildered as the rest of mankind. The important priority is not blame but cure. Once our comments about slavery to communism are out of the way, we devote all our attention to that problem.

Part IV

THE SLAVERY TO COMMUNISM

CHAPTER 14

From Böhm-Bawerk to Objective Economics

It is true as I said at the beginning of Part III that Marx spoke to the hearts of the intelligentsia if not the proletarians in his *Manifesto of the Communist Party*. Stripped of later events and interpreted with some charity, the Manifesto was a noble enough beginning fitting for the young scholar who had previously written his *Theses on Feuerbach*, a book that did much to formulate the meaning of scientific as distinct from other types of knowledge. That nobility was not to last, however, for as the communist doctrine penetrated society first through the efforts of Marx and Engels then Lenin and finally Stalin, matters of the heart were to recede and be replaced by astounding forays into tyranny and brutality.

Even in Marx's own lifetime the tide had turned. Justified in bursts of hatred such as the world had rarely known there were virtually no depths of deceit to which Marx (and Engels) would not and did not sink to promote their views, depths ranging from obfuscation, to lies, to planted book reviews under fictitious names. Well may Mazzini have said of Marx, "Hatred outweighs love in his heart".[62]

Of Lenin perhaps the less said the better. No man ever used to better avail a theoretical edifice that was full of logical inconsistencies to justify almost any course dictated by practical politics. He was a master of such eclectic pragmatism long before a closed railway carriage went from Zurich across Germany carrying him and a score or so of fellow revolutionaries to their ultimate victory in St. Petersburg. Of Stalin, who taught the world new lessons in barbarism, Khrushchev, no amateur himself in the arts of Tiberius, has perhaps said what needed to be said although anyone who thinks the barbarism ended with Stalin need only read the facts of the life of Solzhenitsyn to begin to weep anew. Surely we need not recount any of these horrors. The admiration of the world is owed to the people of Russia for surviving subjugation to such monsters. Although it is early to judge Mao, perhaps we should hold admiration for the people of China for the same reason.

Recoiling from these facts as we must, we must not lose sight of another: that communism, despite the brutes who brought it into the world, is, at heart, an economic doctrine. It is a claim to understanding how economies work just as the subjective economics is such a claim and just as the Objective Economics of this book is such a claim. Whether communism's claim is correct or incorrect, the tenure of its regimes of power in Russia, China, and Cuba can perhaps be explained by brutality of a Calvin-like elect,[63] for raw power can be and is a convincing argument and one of remarkable longevity. The international *marketing thrust* of the doctrine, however, draws nothing but weakness from that brutality. It draws its strength from the doctrine. It is therefore to the doctrine we must address our attack.

It was the Austrian subjective economist Böhm-Bawerk, who was 32 when Marx died and, later, the Austrian Minister of Finance in the tumultuous period 1900-1904, who most directly contradicted Marx's thesis. He did so, however, from the point of view of a subjective economics which we now know to be irrelevant to how economies work. Although Böhm-Bawerk's attack persuaded many of the intelligentsia to drop Marxism it clearly failed to stem the tide. In view of the failure of his own economics to demonstrate relevance, this failure is not surprising.

Böhm-Bawerk's failure has of course made our task of attacking Communism from the sturdier base of Objective Economics more difficult. We must contend with both doctrine and a fait accompli. In Böhm-Bawerk's day, Marx's communism or as Marx preferred to call it, "scientific socialism", was only a revolutionary doctrine. It had enslaved no peoples except for audiences to insufferably long speeches. Despite the scare of the first and abortive Russian revolution in 1905, even as late as the 1917 revolution in Russia, few would have given it much chance of doing so. That it has done so, however, is palpable, and that it is far from confined within a few borders is as evident today as it was in 1953 when Stalin died. Our task, therefore, is rather greater than that of Böhm-Bawerk who pointed out technical error as he saw it but did so from the perspective of an irrelevant doctrine of his own. We not only must point out error as Böhm-Bawerk attempted to do; we also must offer some explanation for the virility of an erroneous doctrine that has risen to power in almost half the world and continues to menace the rest.

In preparing the way for our attack on Marxism or communism I think it is well for us to be aware of the historical context in which Marx wrote at least in very broad terms and at least in terms of economic doctrine. The French Physiocrats led by François Quesnay, and then the Scot, Adam Smith, gave the study of the economy major boosts in the last quarter of the 18th century. Both found that there was a hard core to economic activity, a set of laws if we will, that led to the conclusion that interfering with that activity as by restrictions upon internal movement of goods in France or by similar restrictions on trade with Britain's colonies appeared to hurt society more than it helped it. Combined with the new relevance industry was finding in principles of physical science, a relevance that underlay the so-called "industrial revolution", such claims led to very strong agitations for less government interference in the economy. In English literature at least these agitations are seen as culminating in the Reform Bill of 1830 in England. The Communist Manifesto was published a scant 18 years later.

Marx was a product of neither French nor English society. His background was basically German although his race was Jewish. The Germany of the day was made up of many small principalities all of them more or less dominated by the Hapsburg-controlled Austro-Hungarian Empire. With or without the Hegelian dialectic I shall mention subsequently, within which unification and hegemony of

Germany were elevated to an international goal, such unification was literally carried on the wind, waiting only upon the demise of the Austro-Hungarian Empire and the rise of a German leader. Neither really happened until near the end of the 19th century and in a sense both had no sooner happened than the First World War created a new Europe.

In a German economic climate beset with a succession of federation schemes, Marx found little to point to as the evils of the modern capitalist society that were supposedly pointing the way to its own destruction. Letting the economy work was simply not what was happening in Germany. Even French society offered scarce pickings because in the aftermath of the Revolution the whole process of first getting rid of Napoleon and then living through both Bourbon and Bonapartist restorations posed digestion problems enough. In England, however, political stability existed and it was under that stability that the Reform Bill became law. In the rush into commerce and industry it is commonly believed that no stone was left unturned to present the poorest possible face to unrestrained economic activity. Even today, the mental picture of that period portrays child labor, sweat shops, robber baronry, and associated evils sweeping the land.[64] These were precisely the evils Marx's pen required. What he could not "document" himself, his wealthy English patron, Engels, documented for him. As Marx's writings got him ejected from one domicile after another on the Continent he finally settled in England where he spent the rest of his life.

The British were in no sense unmindful of the problems unbridled economic activity had created. The same 16 years between the Reform Bill and the Communist Manifesto saw the publication, also in 1848, of John Stuart Mill's *Principles of Political Economy*. In many respects Mill may be said to be the father of the modern subjective economics. Not only in that book but also in his *Utilitarianism* and his *On Liberty*, Mill addressed the evils to which Marx was responding. Mill's major social doctrine gave a pause to the thesis of unbridled activity of the economy for he argued that although the laws of production were fixed, the laws of distribution were not. The notion of a "distributive society" in which government plays the role of redistributor was in fact Mill's theme and one that obviously dominates most countries in at least today's western world. In fact it is not a bad reading of doctrinal input to the last 125 years of economic history to say that the distributive society of the western world which we owe to Mill has been poised against the communist society of the eastern world which we owe to Marx. Both, the latter much more violently than the former, are reactions to the unfettered activity of economies advanced by the Physiocrats and Adam Smith. Both see government as central to their scheme. Both involve special technical visions of how economies work, that of Mill being essentially the subjective vision rejected in Parts II and III, and that of Marx lying before us in this chapter. We shall, of course, reject it as well.

It is with some hesitation that I face the task of trying to redirect us to the optimism which characterized the world of Quesnay and Smith—to the effect that interfering in some massive central sense in economies is not the path to human betterment. We are now several generations launched into seeing government, be it communist or not, as having special responsibilities in the economy. That view is so pervasive that, given today's high divorce rate, it may be more strongly believed in than the sanctity of the home. I am all too aware that anyone who even hints at the desirability of a return to the "bad old days" before such initiatives were taken is immediately dismissed as a right-winger and there the argument stops. I can only say that Objective Economics does bring new argument and, different from Quesnay and Smith (and for that matter, Marx and Mill), it also brings startling and even frightening evidence of the argument's relevance. Much of the argument has already been presented as it relates to subjectivism. Let us now turn to Marx's peculiarly inept form of "objectivism".

CHAPTER 15

The Economic Doctrines of Communism

There are six broad subjects within which we can organize the communist interpretation of the economy. They are:

— the materialist conception of history;

— the vision of history as a struggle of classes leading to new class struggles;

— the claim that commodities exchange in the ratio of the "socially necessary labor" they contain;

— the doctrine of an exploitative surplus value;

— the doctrine that the tendency for surplus value to increase leads to an Industrial Reserve Army of Unemployed; and

— the so-called "Law of Capitalist Accumulation" which implies that large capitalists devour smaller ones.

These six theses led Marx to the claim that history tends toward an allegedly great day of take-over by the masses (the proletariat), when "the expropriated become the expropriators".

It is broadly true that all six of these doctrines receive direct or indirect mention in the 8,000-word *Manifesto of the Communist Party* that Marx and Engels wrote in 1848. None of them, however, was argued out in any detail as far as we know until the publication of *Capital* by Marx in 1867. In short, Marx and Engels *believed* all these bold claims for almost 20 years before there is any real evidence that they were substantive deductions or discoveries. This is a shocking example of making up one's mind first and then selecting facts to support that conviction. In spite of his firm grasp of scientific methodology Marx gave many manifestations of just such a procedure over his lifetime.

The materialist conception of history is essentially the claim that man's viewpoint on virtually all important questions is determined by the economic circumstances of the age in which he lives. It is a denial of man's ability in any general sense to rise above and beyond the beliefs required to support the economic institutions surrounding him. For our purposes it is important only to distinguish between this allegation of "unfreedom" for mankind and our allegation in Chapter 2. The difference between our view and his is that we do not say that man *is not* free and we certainly do not say that man's beliefs reflect the economic institutions of the day. We say that it is not relevant *for scientific purposes* to say either that man *is* free or that his views are relevant, because we discover evidence of relevance of the law of constrained fall to states of least economic energy no matter what man believes or tries to achieve. Marx, in short, plays God. We are scientists.

To be more specific, Objective Economics claims no historical insight except to assert two claims that we hold have always been and always will be true because we can point to no exceptions to them. We claim that obligations have been, are, and always will be met, if only by the creditor. We seem not to be able to look beyond that claim and see an exception to it. We also claim that money, whatever it may have been, is, or may be, has no magical properties such as an ability to generate credit from zero balances or an ability to be discounted without revealing a mirror image of accumulation. We seem not to be able to look beyond these claims for when I sell an immature debt owed to me at a price that is discounted below its face value, the person who has bought it has acquired that discount as an accumulation that carries the price he paid up to precisely the face of the debt. This is so because the essence of exchange is the equality of what I sell and my buyer buys.

Such assumptions are historical perspectives if we will. Clearly, however, they make no claims about how people think either about themselves or the institutions surrounding them. They are truths we can abstract from economic activity no matter who the actors are and no matter what the "system" is under which they live. For example, thinking of our second claim, if that system involves no discounting then it involves no accumulation; no exception to the second claim is implied. Thinking of our first claim, if the system were a feudal order in which the nobility entered into no obligations and pressed through life always taking and never giving, then whatever it took was an obligation "honored" by the creditors from whom it was stolen. That is consistent with our first claim.

With his materialist conception of history Marx made no effort, as we have done, to examine history and extract from it what appears to be true beyond reasonable argument. He examined history, accepted some facts, rejected others and finally emerged with history written the way he wanted to see it. In general, the facts he accepted were the sufficiently obvious facts of man's general helplessness if viewed for short life spans to affect the economic activity around him except in a few startling cases that were the exceptions that proved the rule. The facts he rejected were myriad. The dream of liberty, dreamed to the total exclusion of how the economy would work when we had it, has existed over the ages and whole societies have been revolutionized by it. The Jewish dream, dreamt in captivity and dreamt in the Diaspora, has perhaps been one of the major world events that has shaped our history. Its economic content is a detail compared with its religious basis and thrust. Indeed when we combine Judaism and Christianity we obtain a historical movement so strong that, as Shafarevich so ably documents, the historical roots of communism can be detected, far predating Marx—and deplorably weak roots they are, never able to support growth of their own without reigns of terror.

The fact is, Marx had need of a particular way to view history because his teacher Hegel had left him a deceptively simple mechanism for keeping history moving forward in a particular way. To use that mechanism, a mechanism of perpetual struggle, in the manner he wanted, Marx had to "free" Hegel's thought from its fixation on the non-economic ideas in man's mind. This he did by replacing those ideas with institutions, economic institutions which like steel balls in a grinding mill ground the whole man down to a powder that Marx could mold as he saw fit. Thus was born the Marxian notion of class struggle.

Thus the doctrine of class struggle is a more profound issue and has much more respectable philosophical underpinnings than has the materialist conception of history, which is to say, the doctrine of economically brain-washed mankind. It cannot be separated from the fact that Marx studied under Hegel, the German philosopher who advanced the notion that history is what is called a "dialectical process" that can be understood as a never-ending struggle of groups representing an Idea and other groups representing a Counter-Idea. Calling the one idea the "thesis" and the other the "antithesis", the historical process manifests itself as a "synthesis" that within itself contains the new thesis and the antithesis.[65] Having claimed that the only significant ideas are those relating to the economy in his materialist conception of history, i.e. those that are "material", Marx simply borrowed the Hegelian dialectical process, "peopling" both the thesis and the antithesis with economic classes allegedly opposed to each other. Hence peasants and landowners comprise two classes struggling against each other, employers and employees comprise two classes in struggle, and so on. The Marxian historical process, therefore, is a succession of syntheses of class struggles that destroyed feudalism, for example, to create a bourgeois society of employers and employees that in turn produced a capitalist society of large employers versus employees, and so on. Socialism, to Marx, was the synthesis that followed from the class struggle inherent (to him) in the capitalist system.

It is the concept of class struggle that yields the vision of the economy whereby it is seen as always containing contradictions. It is no accident that it was the supreme and ruthless pragmatist, Lenin, who conceived the class struggle in terms of inherent contradictions. It is also no accident that Mao, a man who had to veer in many directions during his rise to power, also saw class struggle in such terms. Neither man could bind himself to a socialism that did not itself contain contradictions, contradictions of policy, even contradictions of doctrine.

There was of course one contradiction that was much too difficult for many of the contemporaries of Lenin to accept. This was the very fact that communism first came to power not in the industrialized west as strict Marxian theory said it should since it was to result from the struggle of capitalists against labor, but in near-feudal Russia. Lenin tried to bridge this contradiction by holding firmly to communism, i.e. the result of the class struggle of industrial workers against capitalists, as a world phenomenon, its actual point of origin being irrelevant. Mao, on the other hand, posed the new doctrinal problem of an alleged communist revolution that sprang not from industrial workers against capitalists, but specifically from peasants against landowners, both of whom were frequently subjugated by local warlords.

Stalin had little patience with such problems of doctrine.[66] For many reasons, once Lenin died, Stalin was faced with creating socialism in one nation and throughout his career he as frequently damaged the cause of world revolution as he helped it. As far as Mao was concerned, Stalin appears to have had great difficulty in taking either him or his brand of communism seriously. Indeed right up to 1948, the year before Mao chased the Nationalists out of China, Stalin was advising Mao to make a deal with them.[67]

This class struggle or contradiction thesis is important enough for my purposes that the next chapter is devoted to it. Therefore I shall not comment on it further at this point.

The next four parts of communist theory, its theory of value, its doctrine of an exploitative surplus value, the claim that an Industrial Reserve Army of Unemployed is necessarily created in a capitalist system, and its law of capitalist accumulation, are all grist for the mill of our Chapter 18, which I have titled, "Intermediation *not* Exploitation Characterizes Economic Life." There are a few comments worth making at this point, however, that will serve to heighten our historical perspective on communism.

It is virtually a cliché of economic literature that Marx took from Ricardo, without reservation, the so-called "labor theory of value", a theory about which Ricardo had severe reservations although much of his economic theory was based upon it.[68] Since that theory gives the utility of items exchanged no weighting whatever in the value equation, it was not an accident that the prominent representative of the Austrian utility point of view to value determination, Böhm-Bawerk, became the best known critic of what Marx had to say about value.

The essential point in this dispute as seen through the eyes of the subjectivists, is that value is not an objective concept that can be freed from the subjective desires and "value systems" of people; nor is it a concept that can be freed of *either* the cost or the utility side of its determination. The Austrians emphasized the latter side. To them, what determined value was the utility that goods exchanged yielded to the exchangers, each of whom gave up a utility in one form for a utility in another form. Marx (and Ricardo) obviously had a problem with a theory based on cost alone, particularly labor cost even when garbled and made circular with the expression "socially necessary", because much of what has price and hence value, items such as virgin lands, ground water, etc., has no labor spent on it. Furthermore, how are we to explain the great differences in price among various types of labor and what can we say about the price of Rembrandt's paintings? Böhm-Bawerk had good fun with these problems and in noting that Marx really was unable to keep utility out of his own statement gave us one of our more vivid metaphors by likening Marx to a conjuror who, wanting to be sure he drew a white ball out of the urn, put only white balls into it.

Although Objective Economics rejects the labor theory of value as does the subjective economics, it claims that the relevant theory of value *is* an objective theory, natural objective value of an entity being essentially the sum of net worth and generated savings of the entity. Since the labor theory of value is also an objective theory in that human choice has little or nothing to do with it, we do have at least the common element of objectivity with Marx in our theory of value. There the parallel stops, because our theory values *entities* rather than the things they exchange. As a result, rather than labor being valued in our theory, it is the labor*er* who is valued since he or she is an entity.

This is an extremely important distinction. Looking at a laborer in terms of his labor totally sidesteps the fact he is also a businessman just as looking at a businessman in terms of his ownership totally sidesteps the fact he is also a laborer. It is only when we look at both as entities, which is to say as balance sheets, that we elevate our sights to a level which frees us from thought structures that are the creatures of our arguments rather than the reverse.

Let us examine the alleged contradictions of economic life, alleged contradictions that in the hands of Marx, Lenin and Mao brought a hatred and a brutality into the world that have set the forces of humanity back at least a half century.

CHAPTER 16

The Contradictions of Economic Life

In this chapter I discuss the contradictions that follow from "ideal" debt structure ratios. As we have seen in Chapter 2, there are powerful forces in the economy that push or pull all entities "as by an invisible hand" in three directions. One forces them ever toward a debt structure ratio of unity, the ratio banks closely approximate. Another forces them to a ratio slightly higher than .80. Still another forces them to a ratio slightly lower than .70.

The first of these forces aimed at a ratio of unity is so molding the entity that its leverage is at a maximum. This means that to the fullest extent possible it is being pushed to a circumstance wherein whatever it borrows it also lends. Thus its "net effect" is to make no credit demands on the economy that it does not satisfy itself and none are made on it that its imaginary counter-entity does not satisfy. Such an entity in the sense of demands on and by the system, therefore, disappears into the mass of entities as if it did not exist.

But operating at maximum leverage contradicts the two other states to which the overvailing law of constrained fall ever pushes it. One of these is the state of least generated savings which obtains when the debt structure ratio is pushed down to slightly below .70.

About the closest we can come to this state with our intuition is to see it as the one that requires the least *working capital* in the total of the entity's lendings as represented by its total receivables and in the total of its borrowings as represented by its total payables. That is, given that one pressure is always trying to equate the entity's receivables and payables and hence to give it maximum leverage, this second pressure creates a division within those totals and tries to minimize one part of that division. It so emerges, however, that the entity cannot have it both ways since for its leverage to be maximal requires a unit ratio, whereas for its generated savings to be minimal requires one just under .70.

There is one way to see this contradiction that is not incorrect although it tells only part of the story. That is to view the pressure for least generated savings as an additional request by the system, namely that demands made on it by the entity should not only be equated by what it brings to the system but that the demands made *right now should always be the least*. Perhaps larger demands can be accommodated later but for the time being the system says "make your least demands today". What least generated savings brings to the economy is, in this view, a type of temporal distortion in which this instant is always special—has a special urgency. This is an important interpretation because Mao made much use of the theme of the urgency of this moment and the fact that that urgency may very well be in conflict with the problems of tomorrow.[69]

Even this contradiction must face yet another. If generated savings are minimal, as the law of constrained fall tells us is one tendency, which is to say, the debt structure ratio is slightly below .70, investment is not minimal. For it to be minimal as that law also requires, that ratio should be slightly above .82.

We can find a way of visualizing the meaning of least investment that, as with our previous remarks about least generated savings, tells only part of the story but is still useful. The requirement that the demands made by the entity on the system *right now* must be least presses upon both total receivables and total payables of the entity. This is the temporal distortion I spoke of previously. As the debt structure ratio changes, not only does the relation of receivables with payables change (for that is what a change in their ratio is), but generated savings, the "burden" itself so to speak, changes. Only at one debt structure ratio is that burden at a value such that when it is distributed over the total receivables and total payables it is supported with the least effort, i.e. the investment is least. That ratio is about .82. At all other ratios the burden is either excessively large or small for one or the other of receivables and payables.

We are talking about bottlenecks. At a ratio of .70, for example, the now demands are excessively high when related to receivables. Doors have to be pounded on to collect receivables in haste while at the same time the actual making of payments is excessively postponed as is the generation of new payables. On the other hand, at a ratio of unity where our leverage is maximal, the now demands are excessively low when related to receivables, and receivables are left out—there is no pounding on doors to collect them. Conversely to this situation on the receivables side, the now demands on payables are excessively high. Like a bank, the entity seeks aggressively for new payables (new deposits) and pays its payables excessively promptly. By tying itself up the least with investments, therefore, it is in conflict with both least generated savings and most leverage.

Thus, if we imagine a world in which no new entities are born, no old ones die and the law of constrained fall has forever in which to work itself out, such world must contain *six* contradictions. Entities pushed to unit ratios have states that contradict least generated savings and least investment. Entities pushed to ratios just under .70 contradict least investment and most leverage. Finally, entities pushed to ratios just over .80 contradict least generated savings and most leverage. Left to its own devices "economizing" yields a peculiarly dynamic outcome that contains contradictions simply because economizing itself cannot make up its mind where it wants the economy to go.

The importance of these contradictions in creating the circumstances Marx found it convenient to emphasize in history cannot be overstated because it is from generated savings, the temporal distortion of economizing to "now" so to speak, that net worth is accumulated. Thus an entity that retains a unit debt structure ratio (as do banks) despite the pressure on it to sample the waters of both .82 and .70, will generate net worth at excessively high pace. In so doing it will find itself leaving its funds out at loan with little effort to bring them in today, and will aggressively borrow new funds to lend. It thus can and will "get the jump" on other entities. If, however, an entity settles at the least investment case at .82 it will find itself making excessive demands on the system by way of its payables. Its net worth will be constantly drained *into* the system in the form of the goods and services the entity produces *for* the system—its production represents this drain. Its generated savings, however, will be above their minimum to compensate for the drain on its net worth. Finally, an entity that settles at a debt structure ratio just below .70 will generate least savings as well as make even greater excessive demands on the system via its payables. It will find too that it is tending always to collect receivables very quickly and to postpone payments and the generation of payables.

It is in these ideal circumstances that we see why banks, i.e. entities that start to "burn" with the fire of credit creation, are born. Both the least investment and the least generated savings cases make excessive demands for payables and are in modalities requiring that their debts lie unpaid as long as possible. Entities that have settled at unit ratio, however, have modalities requiring the opposite. As a result, the springing to life of banks acts like a bridge that allows us to walk from unit ratios to those of .82 to those of .70 without falling into the gaps between them.[70]

Lenin was very perceptive of this powerful role of banks. He claimed that if he could control the banking system he could control a country. Objective Economics allows us to see why this is so. The banks in fact act as counterbalances to entities driven by the law of constrained fall into making excessive demands for payables on the system.

More than this, however, the fact that entities often outlive many human lives allows net worth aggregations that over time are enormously different from the tiny differences our law of conservation ascribes to these values of debt structure ratios. Sometimes such aggregations are via blood lines. More frequently they are the result of economic forces at work that blend entities together. To understand these processes I must introduce further and more powerful grounds for contradiction than those tied simply to the debt structure ratio. They consist in the relation of what I call the "ownership structure ratio" to the debt structure ratio.

CHAPTER 17

Ownership Structure Ratios[71]

It will be recalled that in Chapter 2 and Appendix I it was shown that debt structure ratios yield a distinct clustering pattern. By extending the TSE300 study to calculate the ratios of net worth (N) plus generated savings (E_t) to the market value of the entity (V), a ratio I symbolize by β, it was found that β also had a distinct clustering pattern. Further, the pattern for β was the same as the pattern for α. That is, *the economy appears not to distinguish between α and β and its law of constrained fall applies to both*.

I refer to the ratio

$$\beta = (N + E_t) / V$$

as the "ownership structure ratio". In it the sum of net worth plus generated savings of the entity plays the role of total receivables of the entity, and market value plays the role of the total payables of the entity in the calculation of the entity's debt structure ratio. The difference in interpretation of β from α is that the net worth plus generated savings of the entity is like a payable owed by the entity *to* its owner(s). In that sense it is a receivable of the owner(s) and the market value (V) is like a receivable to those buying ownership in the entity in the market. In that sense it is a payable *of* present owners. The ratio α on the other hand is the ratio of receivables and payables of the entity without reference to ownership.

It is important that we not get tied up in the meaning of words in examining this new ratio and in so doing lose sight of the basic point. That point is that the economy in the operation of its laws *does not distinguish between debt and equity, between liability and ownership.*[72] In other words just as the economy sees creditors paid out so it sees owners paid out. It does not distinguish between the two activities, our evidence of that fact being that it exerts the same pressure on β to rise or fall to our three extrema cases as it does on α.[73]

It follows from these considerations that all of what was said in the previous section about the contradictions re the debt structure ratio can be said re the ownership structure ratio. Powerful forces exist driving that ratio to a unit value. If they win, however, then such entities are in ownership states that contradict both least generated savings from ownership and least investment from ownership. If, on the other hand, the powerful forces driving entities to either of these two extrema win, then two other conditions are contradicted. Clearly, just as we had six possible contradictions with the debt structure ratio, so we have six with the ownership structure ratio.

But now we have a new species of problem. This is the overall contradiction of the debt structure ratio going one way and the ownership structure ratio going another. Let us consider the implications under a separate heading.

The Contradictions of Debt and Ownership Structure Ratios

With the law of constrained fall working continuously on both of these ratios, we have before us an extremely complex technical problem in trying to determine where the economy is headed, i.e. at which ratios it tends to settle if left alone long enough. When we include the law of objective valuation which tells us that, at least in the aggregate, net worth plus generated savings of both entities and ownership should tend to equal their market value, our problem is made even more complex. This is because owners are themselves entities; as such they have owners, and so on in infinite regress.

Such complexities are beyond the scope of this book. However, I do wish to identify as many as possible of the facts of history and the passing scene that Marx-Lenin-Mao found convenient to include in their assertion of *the* historical process, which facts we can explain by incomplete adjustment processes in this complex domain of interaction. It is important to us as scientists that we not interpret such facts as the basis of a historical process, for as the actual process unfolds we will be proven wrong. It is even more important to us as persons of integrity that we not do so because in so far as we hold concern about society and try to influence it we will lead it astray as I believe Marx-Lenin-Mao have done.

First let us consider the struggle that is alleged to be going on between workers and owners. The cockpit of their struggle is of course the company or entity the owners own and for which the workers work. In modern industry this simple picture is complicated by a management group that, although part of the workers, is ordinarily distinguished from them by various owner characteristics, such as profit participation, equity participation, etc., as well as a more direct and intimate connection with owners.

Demands by workers for more wages or other cost-bearing benefits either reduce the company's receivables or increase its payables and if successful usually do both at least at the outset. Thus, the debt structure ratio of the entity falls. If it falls below our conservation range (less than .50) the company develops banking problems which force upon it more and more priority to its collection of existing receivables relative to the priority of regenerating them, and more and more priority to *not* paying payables relative to the priority of *not* regenerating them. Of these four, the priority for *not* regenerating payables is probably the most important since as that priority falls the services of workers are more and more replaced by the services of capital that can be paid out over a longer period. Of almost equal importance is the relative loss of the priority of regenerating receivables. This is usually represented by increased selling prices for the company.

Successful wage demands that force the company beneath our conservation range, that force on it labor replacement by longer pay-out capital, and that force on it higher selling prices, create higher generated savings for the company. This increases the ownership structure ratio in the first instance since that ratio is the ratio of net worth plus generated savings to market value. We know, however, that the forces of constrained fall, which always exist, stop that ratio from moving above our conservation ranges. Those forces act to raise the market value of the company (the denominator of the ownership structure ratio) and hence the rise of β is impeded and finally pushed back. The effect on owners of such increased wages and deepening of capital, therefore, is that the value of their company has risen more or less in step with the resulting increase in their net worth plus generated savings.

Thinking of all labor making such demands together in all companies in concert we can see immediately that the effect of their efforts would help, not hurt, *both* owners and the laborers left employed. On the other hand it would hurt those laborers thrown out of work and the consumers who bought the output of the entities in the economy at increased prices but who were not themselves sellers. *Thus, the problem is not that labor and owners are in opposition but that employed labor is in opposition to unemployed labor, and buyers (who are not sellers) are in opposition to sellers who are also buyers.*

If we think of this process of increased wages going on long enough we see that the "army of unemployed" that is being created by the deepening of capital comes more and more to be the consumers who are not also sellers. Thus, the army of unemployed becomes the very entities who have to absorb the higher prices. Their debt structure ratios have fallen so drastically, however, that they cannot meet existing obligations let alone new obligations following from price rise. Further, as they sell net worth to meet obligations and therefore impede the fall in their debt structure ratios, their ownership structure ratios fall also. They thus become more and more in the position of a company with a high stock market valuation relative to its net worth plus generated savings.

We know that strong forces exist that impede the fall in the ownership structure ratio. Their effect is to place the unemployed increasingly into degrees of "bondage" whereby they have sold part of their ownership of themselves just as a company with a very high and rising stock market value relative to its net worth plus generated savings will at some point sell part of itself by selling new stock from Treasury. The mechanism whereby this happens for the army of the unemployed, setting aside intrusions by government, is that as their full employment by the companies is switched to lesser and lesser degrees and finally zero degree, their receivables that are owed by the companies to them come more and more to be matched by payables they owe to the companies. This is the "company store syndrome" familiar to share croppers in the southern United States. In effect their companies take on banking properties by annihilating obligations in that manner. In short, the company store syndrome waxes and wanes as the ability of companies to raise prices to the army of unemployed waxes and wanes. This is comparable to banks dumping dollars or raising interest rates on existing demand loans as consolation prizes when accounts disappear quickly via chequing flows.

In all of this we are confirming what every businessman and every laborer knows instinctively. The outcome of a concerted rise in wages carried forward forever is the company store as a staging camp that emerges finally into an underfed, totally rejected "army" of unemployed. The paradox, however, that Marx-Lenin-Mao cannot answer is that throughout the whole tale, much of which has happened at various times in history, we find no antagonism between employed labor and owners. There is no "class struggle" between them and no reason why there should be. Further, it is difficult to see how any common element remains between the employed and the unemployed. If there is an antagonism, that is where it would appear to rest. It certainly does not rest between owner and employed labor.

But we cannot stop with the company store as the apparent end product of an army of unemployed. As the wages of the employed rise their receivables and probably their payables rise. As a result, even if their debt structure ratio remains relatively fixed, their ownership structure ratio rises because of the rise in their generated savings as well as net worth. Relative to what the market says those individuals are worth, some of those net worths can now support the waiting entailed in founding a business.

We know that that increase in their ownership structure ratio is more and more impeded and finally reversed. Its rise is represented by movement of more and more labor from relative non-ownership to relative ownership. In fact a larger proportion of employed labor becomes a participant in the generated savings and net worth of existing companies and many who do not thus participate start new businesses.

This introduces what appears to be a new conflict, that between owner and owner which begins as owner vs new owner but finally is general across the whole of the economy. The cockpit of this action is not the company per se but rather the marketplace in which the army of unemployed is walking around disconsolately or is "moving 16 ton . . . owing its soul to the company store." New owners, who usually start out with relatively low debt structure ratios, even if they have bought out old entities whose ratios have crept up, absorb much of the unemployed even though in so doing they probably pay lower wages than the employed are getting. As the unemployed are absorbed they become picked up in the overall drive for higher wages and the whole process starts over at a larger scale. In the end, therefore, i.e. infinity, there is no army of unemployed, there is no owner versus labor class struggle, there is not even an owner versus owner class struggle because today's new owner is yesterday's laborer who is the buyer of what today's owner has to sell, namely his ownership.

The economy left to its natural laws is therefore not a domain of competition and suppression. It is a vibrantly dynamic interplay of processes that tend always to make the present demand the least of the future, subject to the constraints that it also tends to make all individuals demand from the system no more than they put into it and that bottlenecks are minimal. The *impressions* of suppression and competition are always present because the economy never does reach its final adjustment in which all such manifestations disappear. Every act that is committed, however, brings into play the forces of constrained fall that continually file off the rough edges of some entities demanding more from the system than they put into it. The same forces file off the rough edges of the entities that demand more than the least required of the future, just as they do of those experiencing bottlenecks from the pressure of the present upon either their receivables or their payables. The balance of money and goods itself reflects the extent to which this filing off of rough edges has in fact happened. When it has all happened, that distinction will itself be lost, which is to say, all goods will be money, or all money will be goods. This is the Nirvana, if such it is, toward which all economies tend, always have and always will. They do this not as a result of class loyalties and class struggles but because class itself always slips away into disloyalty just as a sandbank finally erodes into the ocean and loses its identity.

Indeed a great deal of the history of communism both as a de facto regime and as a political religion carried by its missionaries has been the construction of semantic masonry to contain the shifting sands of class loyalties of the moment. That is why communism has almost totally rejected all forms of worker participation in ownership, why the variety and quality of the goods produced has been rigidly controlled and is scoffed at in countries where it is not controlled. That is why unions such as Solidarity in Poland pose such a threat because if unions and entity management are able to negotiate in the absence of government they will discover they hold more in common than they do as separate groups. Government, if left out of those negotiations, will find itself the first member of the army of the unemployed. This was a lesson learned very early by Lenin and taken to heart by Stalin. One of the first problems faced by Lenin was to destroy the power of the very unions that were instrumental in bringing him to power. Again and again, in the Ukraine, in the Caucasus, Stalin was faced with the same problem. The problem is not the loyalty within the union. It is that if the union is successful in its demands it will create new disloyalties within itself. Those disloyalties, which begin with slight differences in ownership and debt structure ratios, can quickly accumulate into an economy more and more unrestrained.

As Adam Smith so clearly understood, no matter how we endeavor to read groupings out of the economy, the "classes" of Marxian semantics, the relevant gradations run in terms of individual entities. What he did not realize, however, is that the scientific workings of the economy do not run in terms of what those individual entities *want* to do but in terms of how their ownership and debt structure ratios stack up against the laws of constrained fall. It is on those ratios the full weight of economic activity falls. No individual, no group of individuals, no government, creates that weight. Its essence is the total of all entities, each of which is owned in various degrees by other entities, which are themselves owned in various degrees, and so on in apparent infinite regress. For this reason, it is by no means evident that that weight is even finite. If it is not, then all individual or grouped initiatives to control the economy or even influence it, no matter how massive, are but insignificant in the sweep of natural economic law.

Let us now leave the fictitious class struggle Marx painstakingly and self-servingly picked out of his vision of world history, and move to his doctrine that the economy, left to its own devices, is exploitative, particularly of labor.[74]

CHAPTER 18

Intermediation *not* Exploitation Characterizes Economic Life

A fundamental claim of Marx that has carried through the whole marketing thrust of communism is that the economy, left to its own devices and not trusted to the tender mercies of a Lenin, Stalin or Mao will exploit labor. That communists make the claim with straight faces is perhaps the greatest deception in history.

The mechanism whereby this allegedly happens is payment to the laborer of less than his labor supposedly produces. He is therefore robbed of the "fruits of his labor" by villainous owners. The quantity those owners expropriate from labor in this way is called "surplus value".

The importance of this concept certainly does not follow from any technical merit it may have. It follows from a view which has spread far beyond the communist camp: that the economy is exploitative in the sense that many individuals will receive less from it than they put in. Consequently, various massive encroachments must be made on the economy by central authorities. Modern socialism, and even its more or less respectable ancestor, Fabianism, give much more than lip service to this allegation. Roosevelt's New Deal with its theme of "soak the rich" supported it. In its name, in Canada, the

New Democratic Party, and much of the Liberal Party joined in justifying encroachment on the economy by government. So strong is this undercurrent of erroneous belief in fact that even political parties thought to be of the right wing—such as Canada's Progressive Conservative Party—often present themselves as knights on white horses riding to the rescue of those whom the natural workings of the economy are claimed to exploit.

Both Marx and the subjectivists have visions of the economy that clear the way for an exploitation debate because both get into the mug's game of attempting to link functionally a labor input and a labor output. The Marxian form of the exploitation concept follows from the fact that in seeing value of the product of industry as determined by the amount of labor in it, he either had to say that capital and land made no contribution to value or he had to translate them into labor in some sense. Setting virgin land aside, i.e. land on which no labor had been expended, Marx did translate capital and developed land into labor and in fact viewed them as a sort of "crystallized" labor. It was labor with this difference from the labor currently supplied: it had been "expropriated" by the owner-capitalist in the form of capital. *Whatever* capital produced, therefore, it was stolen from labor because the capital had been expropriated. The subjectivists, by comparison, do not view value as determined by labor content in products, but rather by demand and supply. Thus labor, capital and land all are said to be compensated for their contribution to product with shares that are imputed back to them from market value. This scenario must make assumptions about the degree of competition that exists in the markets for labor, capital and land, and for products. If competition is less than perfect for any of these markets then either laborers or capitalist-owners can exploit either one or the other and the consumer. Unions are seen as monopoly influences that tend to allow labor to exploit owners and consumers just as business cartels are alleged to exploit labor and consumers. In a sense, therefore, both Marx and the subjectivists see the economy as always on the brink of exploiting some groups. Unless regulated in specific ways, it will exploit. Marx's view of exploitation differs from that of the subjectivists in that his is a special case (that of owner monopoly of labor) whereas theirs is the general case. To both, however, the tendency is a prima facie case for encroachment on the economy by a central government.

The essential we learn from Objective Economics is that the valuation process does not in a relevant scientific sense value labor, capital, and land as "service inputs". It values *entities* all of which involve both ownership in the form of net worth plus generated savings which is valued by the economy, and all of which involve processes of being owed receivables and owing payables.

The mode of activity of such a valuation system is, by its nature, neither competitive nor suppressive. It is intermediational. By that term I mean that all entities, laborers, owners, and companies themselves are both laborer and owner in mixed degree. Depending upon the conflict between their debt and ownership structure ratios and the law of constrained fall, they switch by imperceptible degrees from the sale of labor to the sale of capital and vice versa. Indeed, so prevalent yet subtle is this phenomenon that I question the scientific usefulness of trying to distinguish the two roles—that of laborer vs that of owner or that of worker vs that of capitalist. I also question the scientific usefulness of attempting to define and identify various competitive structures. In the world of intermediation, laborers, capitalists, and degrees of competition wax and wane as products of the system.

The important question is not whether owners can exploit labor or labor owners, or whether both can exploit the consumer. There are, in fact, many important questions. Why do many individuals and many companies lack the strong connections that are basic to the overvailing role of intermediation? Why at any given time are many people, each one of whom has a capital of skill of many levels and a potential to acquire more, connected within the economy by very weak threads and sometimes no threads at all? Why do those skills go to waste? Why is it, as Jesus sings in *Jesus Christ Superstar* that "the poor will always be with us"? Why is there always an underworld of companies going belly-up in bankruptcy? Are these weak trading connections within the economy a product of the workings of its laws and if they are does that mean there always must be a class of economic orphans so to speak? These are important questions because in being able to point to the poor, the brutalized, Marx was able to give, and communists are still able to give, credibility to an exploitation argument that could not and cannot be given technical acceptance. The untruth of the surplus value doctrine as a scientific statement pales in importance beside the reality of poverty. There is great truth in the cliché that "poverty is the breeding ground of communism."

The rise and fall of entities as part of a biological necessity of individuals is itself part of the explanation for this phenomenon. As Alfred Marshall so clearly saw, new workers, new companies, struggle into their trading connections by establishing track records. That often implies many years of trial and error and many never establish themselves. Old entities on the other hand often lack the will to struggle and events they would have survived when younger can prostrate them.

These phenomena are not without their benefit to other more established entities. There is no doubt that the "business Methuselahs" of the General Motors, US Steel types gain new leases on life by buy-out, and by simple inheritance from such casualties. Such entities are themselves not immune to failure and they tend to be surrounded by operations that are sloughed off periodically much as a tortoise gets rid of its shell.

What is important in this rise and fall, formation and break-up of entities is that the trading connections within the economy retain their sanguinity in adapting to them. Thus, if persons or entities are allowed by those connections to try only once to establish themselves before being relegated to a cash and carry basis, the slag heap of those who are weakly connected with the economy can grow very large indeed and quickly.

It is here that the credit-generating agencies in the economy, chiefly the banks, are fundamental. In the most vital manner, they create the energies that power the whole system of rise and fall of entities. Any influences acting in the economy to stop them from playing the role of waiting just a little longer than others can or will wait for their money, influences that force them to move credit around rather than generate it, or raise rates on existing credit rather than generate it, destine larger and larger parts of the economy to poverty. They do this because those entities struggling up to strength are killed prematurely as it were, and those that are dying are also killed off too soon. Such phenomena do make the big and successful get bigger and more successful. I have argued strongly in Part III that the insolvency of modern government in the western world has forced the banks into such action modalities. That insolvency, therefore, is a powerful force creating the very circumstances in which communism breeds.

We must not be deluded into thinking of poverty as having an absolute meaning and, having once defined the "poverty level", sticking out our chests because a growing percentage of the people may be above it. It is not only a relative concept but it cannot be related to material things in any scientifically relevant manner. A laborer who cannot achieve the trading connections necessary to become a business person is poverty-stricken from the point of view of economic law just as surely as is one who cannot earn enough to eat. For us to deny that is to make a judgement the economy itself will not make. It is not for us, either as individuals or as governments, to try to ensure that certain minimum standards are met as we define them. It is for us to ensure that trading connections are not so led by the nose by one or two major insolvencies that there is neither time nor place for the mass of the people.

Marx, Lenin, Stalin, and least of all Mao, had little conception of the money market, of the great potential it offers in an economy free of insolvencies for all individuals to grow from weak trading connections into strong ones. That does not mean that a potential exists in such an economy for everyone to be what they want to be and do what they want to do. Wants are not of the essence. Even activities are not of the essence. What is of the essence is the ever-present fact of alternatives. Whatever vicissitudes face us, as long as money markets are made we never quite face a stone wall. This, to me, is the essence of freedom. It is both contemptible and laughable even to suggest that the catechism of Marxism with its eclectic misreading of history, its fallacious class struggle, its lying allegation of exploitation, contains within it a relevant observation about freedom. The word slavery has been used in only three cases with any international orientation in the past 50 years. One was in Hitler's Germany. A second persists in parts of Africa and the Middle East. The third dates from practices begun by Stalin in the 1930's, practices that appear still to exist in the Soviet Union and its satellite countries. In point of numbers of the truly enslaved in all of history, there are certainly those who believe that, were the facts known, Stalin's essays in the field of slavery far exceed any others of like duration. In the next chapter I try to identify the nature of another type of slavery associated with communism that is to me the basis of its international marketing thrust. We can do nothing for the hordes of people Stalin and his successors have enslaved. We can do something to try to stop any further spread of that slavery.

CHAPTER 19

The Nature of the Slavery to Communism

The nature of our slavery to inflation is, as stated at the end of Part III, an information flow made necessary by the insolvency of central governments that enslaves us and has become critical. Man has had to become a computer and in doing so he has become a slave.

The nature of our slavery to communism in non-communist countries is vastly different. It has little effect upon the level at which our economies operate and even less upon our day-to-day business activities. Instead of impinging upon us at these levels it conditions the way we think of the economy and in so doing has much to do with our expectations about what the economy can do for us. In this, communism joins the major religions that have been thrust upon mankind over the centuries, for they too have conditioned our thinking about the economy.

I think the word "contempt" is an adequate description of the reaction communism has given us to economic events and the workings of the economy. Religions were more likely to make people run to their caves and hide in fear from thunder and lightning than to make them embark upon a study of electricity. In much the same way, communist thought forms have made us throw up our hands

hands and ask "what can you expect?" when we have been confronted with economic events that fix our attention.

In teaching us contempt for the economy and preaching that if we do not master it, it will master us, communism received a major assist from John Maynard Keynes. Working with totally indefensible aggregative concepts of the economy, Keynes claimed in his *General Theory* to have shown that, left to its own devices, the economy would not necessarily achieve full employment. It would, in his jargon, reach equilibrium at less than full employment. With the discoveries of Objective Economics in hand we dissent from Keynes' thesis not on the grounds that his reasoning was wrong but on the grounds that employment and unemployment just do not happen to be categories or quantities in terms of which the economy, *conceived scientifically*, manifests its activity. What Keynes really did was to show us his contempt for the economy by saying implicitly: "*I* know the concepts in terms of which the economy works, and what economics is going to be about is the interrelations of those concepts." Communism has done the same thing. It has said: "Economies operate in terms of groups exploiting other groups and in so far as studying the economy is worth the effort at all, that study will simply document how those groups interact to create their successors." Both views are contemptuous of the economy as a system of laws we may be able to discover. Both views play God.

I hope I have communicated to the reader that such approaches differ fundamentally from that of Objective Economics. It makes two assumptions that seem virtually impossible to deny: the assumption that all obligations are met if only by the creditor, and the assumption that money has no magical properties. Having made those assumptions it then proceeds to extract their implications. In so doing we discover the concepts in terms of which economies appear to work. They include neither the Keynesian aggregates nor those of Marx. Indeed, both Keynes and Marx, in the insights of the new science, are Merlins in pointed hats conjuring up visions of a netherworld to which they are welcome.

Nothing will break the slavery of contempt for the economy that we have acquired from Marx and Keynes faster than the humility we learn by testing our science against reality. That is why throughout this book I have emphasized the TSE 300 study. The tests of that study are exciting. They also are humbling for they tell us there is a world unknown out there. They tell us we are just starting to make a few halting steps to understand it. They also tell us that much of the method by which we have gained scientific purchase of physical reality will be useful to us and make us bolder.

This is extremely important because the one thing the brutes who sired communism could not do was let their people slip backwards in physical science. It is my hope and my suspicion that in that necessity we find a way from west to east that penetrates the Iron Curtain. Major mathematical problems are posed by Objective Economics and the dimensionless science of observation of which it is a part. Many thinkers will be required both to state and solve them. I believe that neither the Marxian catechism, nor the Leninist political eclecticism, nor the Stalinist brutality, nor the Maoist dogmatism will be able to stop some of the communist world's great intellects from involving themselves in those problems.

PART V

PASSIVE RESISTANCE TO INSOLVENT GOVERNMENTS

CHAPTER 20

The Moment of Truth

And so we come to the moment of truth—our creed. We have travelled a long road with many detours. We have had to absorb much that is new. We have been asked to reevaluate and actually value much that is old and has been largely rejected in this world of academic brilliance that allegedly surrounds us. That world, we have found, is not as brilliant as it is presumed to be. In fact, had we followed the untutored wisdom of our ancestors, our descendants would be looking at better days. Instead of ending our review by discovering who the villains are, we have found ourselves unable to identify them. Not villainy has been the enemy, but ignorance. Its handmaiden has been acquiescence in subverting the disciplines of the system.

In one sentence, *we must stop cooperating with insolvent governments by allowing them to subvert the disciplines of the system, and we must, through that resistance, force them to bale themselves out by privatization rather than theft.* "Don't come to me for loans until you have sold enough assets to show that you are a worthy borrower" must be society's response to modern insolvent government. As we advance that response, however, we must also say and insist the message be heard, that government is not to retreat one inch from the responsibility to govern. Over millennia society has progressively deposited its liberties with governments it elects and for the most part it has been well served by them. This is a tradition we must not allow governments to take from us and we must not take it from them. The issue is neither more nor less government. It is *better* and more powerful government with *less*.

The term "society" is a modern euphemism that often comes close to referring to nothing in the real world. It is not *society* that must force this creed upon government. It is people, sometimes individuals, sometimes groups of individuals, sometimes individuals hidden within corporate structures that conceal individuals. The final chapter, our "how to" chapter, is aimed at all those people and groupings thereof.

Inevitably, responsibilities do not fall equally. The money market professionals, be they bankers, brokers, insurance companies, or pension fund managers, probably have the heaviest responsibility of all. That responsibility is so heavy that those professionals, if they are to gain the confidence to act, will need the urging and the conscious support of individuals and groups of individuals that are important to them in carrying out their functions.

The risks of "going it alone" in resisting insolvent governments are simply too great to countenance. Fortunately all professionals in the money market have close inter-dependencies. As a result it is possible for the consensus we require to grow across the whole market quickly.

Of all these professionals, the pension fund managers and the brokers strike me as the most vital links for starting the passive resistance ball rolling. From the former, with whom the latter hold a close dependency, a type of long-sightedness is required. From the brokers a combination of creativity and courage is required from an industry that would never have existed had it not originally possessed those qualities. I am extremely anxious to persuade these two parts of the business community to activities that measure up to and perhaps even exceed the call of duty.

In an earlier chapter, I said people commit suicide; governments do not. I think I have been overly callous in that assessment, which implied that government would not assist us in passive resistance to itself. I have never met a politician I felt was a bum or a scoundrel.

Quite to the contrary, it has been my experience that political life attracts people of high ideals indeed. I think it is not overly sanguine to expect considerable assistance from government with our program once it is understood. Much of the "Reagan-rhetoric" could and probably does conceal friends and not enemies of our program and there is no doubt that that rhetoric finds a world audience among governments.

I suppose it is inevitable that a creed that tells government to wind-down and sell-off will appeal to the "right" much more quickly than to the "left". On serious reflection, however, I believe the organized labor movement, even those parts assumed to be of the left, will become a strong supporter of our creed. The reason this is to be expected is that protection of assets is every bit as crucial a problem to modern unions as it is to trust companies and banks. Our creed tells us nothing negative about wage levels; in fact no blame has been levelled at wages in this book as a cause of inflation. [75]It tells us a good deal, however, about protecting assets. I look for much curiosity leading to cooperation from organized labor.

Both communism and socialism will die pari passu with the death of the subjective economics. All three are based upon the same misunderstandings of how ALL economies work and none can survive the birth of an objective science of those workings. Who owns what has never been the issue. The issue has always been that, whatever they own, owners cannot be insolvent or we all are hurt. The international marketing of a hard-headed, brutal communism, the practice of a soft-headed banal socialism, and the sophistry masquerading as the science of subjectivism used in advising most western governments, will all undoubtedly try to "tough it out". All three, however, are caught in the mesh of vastly increasing the complexities of economic life, of causing us to plan the unplannable, of locking up our precious economic energies in ways from which they can never be retrieved. Passive resistance to governments actively influenced by them can overcome in all three cases. Communist governments in place, however, as distinct from their international marketing of their creed, will not have the luxury of such bloodless transactions. Minimizing the imminent sufferings of their people as communism goes through its death throes is a first priority and one of which the current Polish scene has made us acutely aware.

Although with some skepticism or uncertainty, therefore, it is with a great deal of hope that I turn to our Manifesto. I believe as well that something else is involved, something else that, in the absence of a word more in keeping with my modes of expression, I shall call love. It certainly is not the hatred that smoldered, for whatever reason, in the breast of Marx when he wrote his Manifesto. I like to feel that none need die in any cause least of all mine. We have killed so many. We have maimed and mutilated so many more all in the name of this or that Promised Land. No piece of dirt has been worth it. Surely the wit of man, the sense of decency in mankind of which we all are aware, even those least willing to confess it, and a little patience, can achieve a great deal for us. I hope so. If I must be naive about something, then that faith is my choice.

CHAPTER 21

Man's Noblest Creation—the Money Market

When I think of the money market, I am reminded of the passage in St. John's gospel about the woman taken in adultery. Jesus said to the scribes and Pharisees: "He that is without sin among you, let him first cast a stone at her." Later, to the woman, he said: "Neither do I condemn thee: go, and sin no more."

I feel that way about the money market. Its debasement through the subversion of its disciplines by central banks has been a sickening event to witness. We desperately need to say to the money market that, despite that Fall, "You are loved, and having sinned once you do not have to continue sinning again and again."

The problem, as very frequently, is one of money.[76] On any given day perhaps a majority of large brokers is preoccupied with the business of central banks keeping their insolvent government clients in the economy. Those brokers own large inventories of debt issues, mainly short-term debt issues of government that they must get out of their hands and into the hands of clients before another load of that paper emanates from the central bank. If they do not sell the paper in their hands on that day, before new paper hits them they must price the new paper lower than the old and, in so doing, increase the rate of interest and cause capital losses to those of their clients who have bought the old paper from them if they sell it before maturity. Such imminent capital losses apply to the brokers themselves for the inventories of paper they hold.

What does this pressure mean in terms of the realities of the day-to-day money market? A large institutional investor who controls a fund well into the billions of dollars told me that on a particular day on which the Bank of Canada was selling a billion-dollar issue of bonds, his office received 18 broker calls in 30 minutes, in all of which his arm was being twisted to buy into the issue. In this hurly-burly of huckstering another fund manager, again one who controls funds in the billions, told me that on a recent similar issue he had purchased over $100 million dollars worth by 11a.m. whereas for almost a year previous he had purchased none of the Bank of Canada offerings. At 11a.m. he received a phone call from a Bank of Canada representative who congratulated him for buying in. He spent the next half-hour trying to find out which of his brokers had given the bank the privileged information that he was a buyer. When he failed to identify the leak he informed all his brokers that the bank had no more right than any other bond seller to know he was in the market and if he ever again found the bank (which is itself a buyer of such issues) being given privileged information he would seek redress at law.

These reports, and they but sample comments many large institutional buyers of paper have given me, bring to the fore a characteristic of government debt that is becoming increasingly alarming to its potential buyers. This is that government debt brought on the market goes through none of the regulatory obstacles that other forms of debt must go through before the services of the money market can be enlisted to sell it. No prospectuses are registered. No statement of what is to be done with the money is made that is worthy of reading. No evidence of solvency for the government borrower is presented. If AT&T, or Noranda Mines, or Houston Natural Gas wish to use the money market to borrow funds, each will spend millions of dollars to ensure that regulations of the market (by the Securities Exchange Commission in the United States or various provincial securities commissions in Canada) are met. Those regulations involve, among other details, complete disclosure of the affairs of the borrower. By comparison, central government debt handled by central banks is sold before the governors or chairmen of those central banks have finished the phone calls in which the terms of the sale are set. Quite possibly the ink is not even dry on the paper itself. Equally possibly, the paper may not even have been printed on the day of the sale.[77]

These facts recount a violation of business ethics by the brokerage community that would send its members to jail if they did it in any other context. They recount a mode of activity by brokers whereby their hard-earned and *true* reputation of scrupulousness in handling other people's money suddenly goes down the drain when they deal with the paper of the most serious insolvencies of all, namely central governments. Why? As I say, it reduces to money. AT&T, Noranda, and Houston Natural Gas have not plugged the brokers' "inventory pipe" with paper that has to be sold willy-nilly, somehow without damaging the price of new paper entering today. Within limits, the broker can wait a few hours, even a day or two, for such issues. He can also offer advice to hold back the issue date of the new paper and usually can take steps to hold it back. With government paper, however, there can be no waiting. Not only are delays infrequent for new government paper; it frequently comes on the market in unexpectedly large chunks as the awareness of cash problems by government suddenly changes.

The great paradox is that this failure of the brokerage industry to apply even the most rudimentary tests to government debt issues follows not from broker venality but from the brokers' attempt to be good citizens. More than a generation of brokers has been brain-washed by that peculiar ignorance promoted by the subjective economics in which central banks are seen not as the architects of inflation, not as agents of insolvent governments that must have them as an addict must have drugs, but as emissaries of the gods who look benevolently down on us earthlings. Central bankers are seen as the real emperors of western economies.

In fact these emperors have no clothes. They are born into the world to perform one task and one task only and if we look closely at them, they do it in nakedness. Their job is to subvert the banking discipline; they do it by fair means or foul but they do it. In their early days they have been in most cases charged with financing governments whose debt structure ratios were falling from 1.0 or there-abouts down to .90, .80, .70. It was at this last value that what appeared to have been working, which is to say, decreases in bottle-necks, and increases in the efficiency of the use of the currency, started to reverse themselves and the ability of the central bank to keep dollars working without bottlenecks started to deteriorate. The damage had already been done to the brokers' objectivity. Faced with the massive stonewalling by central banks of the image they projected as having some beneficial role in the economy, the brokers (I think reluctantly) agreed and began to play the central banking game. Yet that game violates both the spirit and the letter of the laws controlling brokers with all other types of paper.

How do we get brokers to stop the game? The answer lies I sug-gest in the hands of the major institutional investors, particularly those that handle the rapidly accumulating pension funds, insurance account funds and so on. No money market dealer can live without some considerable access to those funds. This is particularly true when government borrowing is the major repetitive *new* borrowing that increases apace and pension funds are the major *new* source of investment money that grows at roughly the same rate. By voluntary agreement among pension fund managers that no exceptions and no exemptions from registering full details of all borrowings would be tolerated if their funds were to go into an offering, pension fund managers could make central banks face the truth almost instantly. They also would relieve the brokers of an enormous moral burden. Virtually no money market dealer (broker) would risk buying a gov-ernment debt issue that had not qualified. A dealer's own capital is so small as to be almost trivial compared with the risk encountered if it could not retail such debt to pension funds. Even if the broker were a "designated broker" under the Purchase and Resale Agreement in Canada, or even if it were a specialist broker dealing extensively with the United States Treasury, no broker would even consider becom-ing the financier of the federal government of either Canada or the United States on its own account. All the brokers must "job" such debt. If they could not do so to various fund managers they would withdraw no matter what the cost.

How do we appeal to fund managers to insist upon such rules? We must solve two problems for them. The first problem is replacing government debt with other paper of at least equal attractiveness. Pension funds grow at such an astonishing rate (some at as much as 30% per year) that they must be invested continually in paper the price of which is not instantly sensitive to that need to invest. The second problem is weaning them away from all sentimental feelings that in buying government debt they are not only doing what is easily defensible to their own peers, but they are being good citizens.

I suggest that it is not beyond the wit of the brokerage industry to design and sell debt issues that are backed by so many corporate borrowers grouped together that those issues can offer more than is offered by government debt. Indeed within the prospectus for such an issue, options could be available that made everything possible from the "instant money" feature of Canada Savings Bonds to the locked up funding of very long term debt.

The design details of such a package, however complex, are not the issue. They can be solved. So too can the problem be solved of pulling a number of large corporate (and perhaps state and provincial government) borrowers together. I can name at least five promoters with all the competence necessary to put the package together and I suspect most readers can themselves name at least five. Putting the package together is not the problem. The problem is to recognize, and cater for, its changing characteristics. What starts out as a debt package, to replace the government debt package that exists currently and amounts in Canada to $14-17 billion in the year of net new debt (as distinct from debt that rolls-over old debt) and several times that in the United States, will tend more and more to become a debt-equity package. This will happen as the brokerage community tries to put together larger and larger offerings that will both satisfy the voracious appetite of fund managers and drive the central banks out of the market. The reason it will happen is the law of constrained fall to states of least economic energy which was developed in Chapter 2. From that law we know that there are limits ever operating in the market that hinder debt structure ratios from falling beneath a central range. Those limits will force upon the brokers who are putting the package together an increasing proportion of equity or "stock" offering in the package. As a result, when the package is put together that can, on the one hand, meet the ever-expanding needs of fund managers for investment opportunities and, on the other hand, drive central banks out of the market, the mix of paper that is available to the fund managers will almost certainly contain much less debt issue than currently exists and a substantial proportion of it will be equity issue.[78]

The question is: "Equity in what?" Clearly the equity would be in what the proceeds of the new issue are to be used to buy. If our goal is to stop inflation what the funds must buy is the assets of government. In short, the essence of putting a package of debt and equity paper together that would be of sufficient scale and quality to satisfy the needs of fund managers *and* drive central banks out of the money market is the buy-out of government assets to the degree required to return it to solvency. This central focus of the whole plan, namely to break the dependence of the brokers upon the central bank activity of creating enough inflation to accommodate insolvent government, is so important that the next chapter is devoted to it in its entirety.

CHAPTER 22

Privatization by Purchase of Government Assets in Space Technology

In this chapter I make a specific recommendation of what government assets should be bought out to create paper, both debt and equity paper, that will on the one hand satisfy the fund managers' appetite and on the other hand drive central banks out of the money market. That recommendation implies a colossal enterprise within which nearly all of the world's know-how re space technology is contained. For reasons given in the following, I believe this enterprise could serve our purpose and defeat inflation. Even if the reader does not agree with its selection, the principles involved remain the same whatever major project replaces it.

Perhaps the one finding of Objective Economics that is easiest for all mankind to visualize is that inflation is caused by the continued existence within the economy of major insolvents. Such existences create all of the stresses and strains that manifest themselves in inflation. Since they can only exist at the expense of the banking discipline it is by examining bank data in relation with the value placed on banks in the equity market that we obtain our most sensitive measure of inflation.

In one way or another many companies sink into insolvency and in so doing "get into the banks" as common language has it. When this happens the sternest of remedial measures are forced upon the company. Very frequently those measures include the sale of some assets and a desperate attempt to save others from sale that are sufficient to keep some semblance of the business alive. Out of the proceeds of sale of assets some of the liabilities are paid out and in the glow of that best effort it is frequently possible to refund others, which is to say, find ways of refinancing them. With a little luck, a lot of faith, and extraordinary effort, many companies make it back into solvency. It is in this manner that economies have "incrementalized" their way out of inflationary pressures since, at any time, the vast majority of entities is solvent and the economy as a whole can absorb those that are not while they work out their problems.

In many respects the whole of this book and of my previous book is the story of how governments, money-issuing governments, were misled into believing that the rules outlined in the last paragraph do not apply to them. We have discovered that they do apply. Although they always have applied, we have discovered that central banks have been able to conceal the workings of those rules by first creating a money market in their own image and then terrorizing it. One effect of that subversion of the banking discipline has been to keep the money market dealing with an insolvency it would otherwise have rejected. The other effect has been all of the manifestations of inflation of which the most relevant is the direct damage to banks. In Part III I showed one of those damages to banks and measured inflation by it. In Appendix III I show another that is even more serious. That is the rapid decline of the net worth share of the natural reserves of the banks. As that share approaches 30% while still falling, one can sense the approach of reversed priorities for banks in total that will dampen down the boilers of credit creation and fire up the boilers of credit collection and postponement of payments.

Coincident with these serious problems is evidence that even the central banks have rapidly run out of steam. In the United States wide and violently fluctuating spreads between the Federal Reserve Board's rediscount rate to the banks and the Federal Funds Rate at which banks borrow from each other have become the rule rather than the exception. In Canada, the sums loaned by the central bank so that brokers can lend to it are ten or twenty times what they were a few years ago. Both phenomena manifest near panic as the central banks try to get a handle on an economy that is ruthlessly rejecting the presence of their governmental client. Central banks cannot even fool themselves any more by closing their eyes to these phenomena. The day is dawning on which they will realize that whereas their original role was to subvert the banking discipline, they have now become the agents of government take-over of the economy as it exercises its option to steal.

Thus, on the one hand we have had a steady rise of central banks to power and then decline to weakness. On the other hand we have had a steady penetration of the economy by government. Both processes have been effected with minimal public display. Both, however, have now arrived at a point at which all the violence and public display of inflation that have accompanied them, and that have not been perceived as related to them by most observers, will be matched and is being matched by equally evident violence by central banks and governments. Last spring (1980) the actions of the Federal Reserve Board when faced with events it neither predicted nor could control were nothing but crass expropriations from financial institutions. The United States Congress has increased the legal power of that Board to carry out its depredations by making it legal for it to accept almost any type of paper in rediscount. In Canada, one of our provincial governments openly accuses the federal government of outright and bold-faced theft in its proposed energy policies. These are violent events. They are but a prelude to the death throes of insolvent governments and of their financial agents who no longer can do their subversive work for them. Those death throes will involve inflation that beggars its own history for violence. The option of incrementalizing bit-by-bit is no longer available. The events that lie ahead if we cannot avert them are catastrophic.

It is against this background that I have selected a specific project of buying out government assets (rather than sitting waiting to be expropriated) that is grand enough in scale to be able to alter the course of these disasters. Very few such projects can be imagined and I am by no means certain that the one I have selected, the sale of space technology, can do the job. Much recommends it, however, and although the reader may have a better idea, the principles underlying the following remarks will apply to any major buy-out project.

CHAPTER 23

The Technical Background of Buy-Out of Government Assets

First, we need to scale the problem of buy-out of sufficient government assets to make government solvent. Since space technology is largely an American property our calculations must be done for the United States. Combining the findings of the stock market study with our knowledge of Objective Economics, our problem reduces to first determining the debt structure ratio of the United States Federal Government and then determining what its net-back would have to be to bring that ratio above .30.

Specifically, the payables of the United States Federal Government are about $1,000 billion. Judging largely from the behavior of the Federal Reserve System and staple reasoning about taxes owing at a given time, I would expect the receivables of that government to be not more than $200 billion. I assume its debt structure ratio, therefore, is .20. That ratio assists me to make an important point, to which I shall return, about the extensive degrading of net worth suffered by insolvents. For that reason, even if the true ratio is somewhat less or more than .20, it is useful to start with that value.

One of the remarkable results of the stock market study is that it allows us to estimate the net worth of government even though governments do not record net worth and do not trade on the market. (Certainly government *bond* issues are traded, but in the absence of prospectuses, mentioned earlier, there is no means of assessing what the issuing entity is worth.) We can make such estimates because even though governments do not trade on the market and do not even show net worth in their books, we can discover their receivables and payables from their books and hence calculate their generated savings. We know from the stock market study, however, that there are specific arithmetic relations between net worth and generated savings for each debt structure ratio.

Making the necessary calculations for the United States Government we find:

(1) Its generated savings are—

$$E_{t(.20)} = (1000+200) \times 10^9 \times [1/m(c)^2 + 1/m^1(c^1)^2]$$

in which $m=40.81$, $c=4.09$, $m^1=57.15$, $c^1=.75$, if its debt structure ratio is .20. We obtain, therefore,

$$E_{t(.20)} = \$35.4 \text{ billion.}$$

(2) The stock market study tells us that when the debt structure ratio is .20, net worth tends to be only 3.3 times generated savings. The current net worth of the United States Federal Government, therefore, is estimated to be 3.3 times $35.4 billion, which is $116 billion.

(3) To raise the debt structure ratio to .30 by sale of assets, assuming that in the sale government receivables are increased by the proceeds of the sale and by the same amount as its payables are decreased, we simply solve for x in

$$(200 + x)/(1000 - x) = .30$$

to obtain $76.9 billion. In short, if the United States Government can come up with a package of assets to sell that will yield it sale proceeds of $76.9 billion and at the same time free it from the same amount of payables, it can pull itself up to a marginally solvent debt structure ratio of .30.

(4) Let us assume human ingenuity and marketing skills are sufficient for such a package to be put together and sold. The

effect would be a new generated savings for the government of

$$E_{t(.30)} = (276.9 + 923.1) \times 10^9 \times [1/m(c)^2 + 1/m^1(c^1)^2]$$

in which m=33.89, c=3.80, m^1=48.09, and c^1=.99. We obtain, therefore,

$$E_{t(.30)} = \$27.9 \text{ billion.}$$

This is a decrease in generated savings from its present state. In other words, the efficiency with which money is used by the government increases.

(5) The stock market study tells us that at this marginally solvent ratio of .30, the ratio of net worth to generated savings is much higher than it is for the insolvent ratio of .20. In fact it is 7.1 as compared with 3.3. The net worth of the government as a result of the sale of assets will therefore be 7.1 × $27.9 billion = $198 billion. Thus, by a *sale* of assets that pulls the US Government up into marginal solvency its net worth will actually *increase* by $198 billion − $116 billion = a gain of $82 billion!

(6) Having achieved a debt structure ratio of .30, let us assume it sells enough assets to pull that ratio up to .50 which we know is not only a solvent ratio but is one at which the private banks are interested in its business. A central bank, therefore, will not be necessary. To achieve this on present assumptions, the government would have to sell $130 billion of assets and, without showing the calculations, I assert that its net worth would jump to $376.2 billion. Thus, by the *sale* of first $76.9 billion and then $130 billion, a total of $206.9 billion, its net worth is *increased* from $116 billion to $376.2 billion, a gain of $260 billion.

The paradox about these calculations, ideal as they may be, is not that by *sale* of assets by an insolvent its net worth increased; *it is that every businessman in the world understands the mechanism.* Net worth rapidly degrades for insolvents as the priorities of the business switch to the stormy waters of insolvency. When we reverse the process by sale of assets it is like sailing into clear water as net worth rebounds. What Objective Economics and our market study allow us to do is to put some numbers around that familiar phenomenon. Those numbers lead to sufficiently impressive findings that the asset-sale route to solvency of government and hence removal of inflation from the economy simply must be examined further. Even if our achievement were half of what this ideal example yields, the exercise would still be worth taking. Let us look at the problem of asset sale by government rather more squarely than I have thus far.

CHAPTER 24

Design of the Asset Package and Philosophy of its Sale

Pushing or prodding insolvent governments to the design stage for a package of assets to be sold is, as I have said in Chapter 21, largely the responsibility of fund managers and brokers. A simple refusal to deal in paper that has not gone through the same due process of information and justification as has all other paper would quickly give a message to all central banks. That message would indicate that the money market had its own "freedom manifesto" and that, although central banks would not be excluded from it, they must comport themselves with the dignity and honesty of all the other players in it.

Even that action by fund managers and brokers could have catastrophic results within weeks, even days. The simple fact that central banks or government treasuries had to document debt issues in a manner comparable with the methods used by AT&T or Noranda Mines could force postponement of pay-out of government bills and that might in turn lead to massive default by government. That is to be avoided at nearly any cost. To avoid it, notices would have to be given. That is, governments and their agents would have to be notified by fund managers and brokers that by a certain date, perhaps six months hence, the new rules would be applied. Until that date it would be "business as usual." That would give government some time to recognize that sale of assets was inevitable but not sufficient time for it to plan and accomplish a massive take-over of private business in the economy.

We would do well to realize that insolvent governments are in their death throes. Although over time I believe wise counsel will prevail, the immediate reaction of government to a money market that refuses any longer to be bullied will undoubtedly be vicious. I can see attempts to take over all major pension funds, attempts to take over private banks, even an attempt to set up government-controlled brokers. As a matter of fact we can expect all of these thrusts and more as the financial community tries to sit the government down in its bankruptcy chair and read it the facts of life. Appeals to a mob that for the most part has no investment at stake will be rife; all the tired slogans of robber barons will be trotted out; all the worst in the demagoguery permitted in a democracy will be elevated to a central role as it has been so many times.

These facts make it all the more urgent that a buy-out proposal be ready and that at every stage it be presented as an alternative. The essence of the bargaining has to be that the hysteria of a government suddenly faced with a fundamental obstacle to its continuance in its present modalities is turned more and more to raising the price of that buy-out offer. This can only happen if the government and the people know what that offer is. We must hope that, as the buy-out offer is continually waved as the alternative, wise counsels within government can start to advance the case that what is really at issue, namely the ability of government to govern, not only is not being diminished; it is or can be increased.

This is the crucial fact. Financial involvement in the economy is not the source of government's power. It is often the source of its weakness. In Canada we have an outstanding example of that fact in Nova, an Alberta corporation. The Government of Alberta has no financial ownership of that company but it does have directors on its board. Those directors, who are in a minority, have for many years been able to communicate the wishes of government to that utility. The government on the other hand has been kept informed of the wishes of the company. Although I am sure there have been many problems between the company and the government, none of them has broken out into the public arena in the way they have for either companies defiantly free from government such as Imperial Oil, or companies such as Canada Development Corporation in which the federal government is the largest, albeit a minority, shareholder.

Financial involvement by government in private business, either as a creditor or as an investor, is not necessary for government to have its say and be heard. Indeed, it can be and often is an embarrassment that weakens government's voice. What is necessary is that the government be informed on major issues in sufficient time that it can act in the interest of the people if necessary. Nova offers strong evidence that that kind of system can work without impairing the company's creativity and freedom to act.

As wise counsels start to prevail in government, the realization will grow that the *sale* of government assets is far from their *abandonment*. In fact, depending upon the creativity with which the sale package is designed, the government involvement with them, its ability to ensure that those assets are used on behalf of the people rather than against the people, can increase. If the package is exciting to business, business will accept government monitoring. If it is more exciting, it will accept not only monitoring but perhaps some specific guidelines. If it is even more exciting than that, it might accept monitoring, guidelines, and certain mandatory types of behavior. These degrees of involvement by the government seller *after* the sale are all part of the bargain. The longer government hysteria lasts once the money market lowers the boom, so to speak, the less that involvement will be.

A great deal depends, therefore, on the design of the package. That is a major reason I believe the sale of space technology in a very general sense of that expression to be a useful focus for the package. Space technology captures the imagination of all of us. Another reason is that, thus far, space technology and most of its hardware are the property of governments, chiefly the United States Government, but also the government of the Soviet Union and, in much lesser degree, several other governments. Even Canada's government has significant properties, particularly in the communications field.

In the United States and a few other countries, is there enough of that technology available to afford a buy-out price of the order of $75 billion and the assumption of debts of the same amount? I expect there is if we define the package widely enough to include all current know-how both civilian and military. In asserting that expectation we must recognize two facts. The first is that what will be paid for the package depends upon its various hard- and software component costs even less than an automobile price depends upon its component costs. The real issue is what private business thinks it can do with the package. The possibilities can be gauged from a brief catalogue of the activities upon which business might focus, such as: solar energy; or global travel; or an advanced cryogenic industry that enters every home; or a personalized communication system; or space travel, space exploration and planetary resource exploitation; or production, biological or mechanical, in a weightless environment; or space warehousing. We can never evaluate these possibilities until pencils are sharpened, great burdens of secrecy are lifted, and project feasibilities are calculated.

The second fact we must realize is that government does not go into these negotiations in weakness. The very fact that the alternative to an acceptable sell-out price can be default is a mighty club to wield over fund managers who already are deeply, and desperately involved in holding government debt. It is clearly true that exchanging that debt or a major portion of it for equity is preferable to facing default. Indeed, if the package were sufficiently exciting, some fund managers would need little convincing. Perhaps I am overly optimistic but I see little difficulty, given a creative package, in the government being able to transfer $75 billion of its debt into equity.

But that is less than half of the problem. There remains the problem that the buyers who would have given up that much equity already as a result of the debt to equity transfer would still have to come up with an additional $75 billion as a buy-out price. Even that does not finish the job. They still have to face the final problem of putting enough money into the new company so that it can operate. For talking purposes, let us assume the funds required to operate are $25 billion. In addition to the equity that has been given up to government bond holders to switch them into equity which we assume frees the government from $75 billion of debt, therefore, a further $100 billion has to be raised by debt or equity. How those funds are raised is crucial.

The deficit of the United States Federal Government is currently in excess of $65 billion. That means that in 1981 that government is borrowing that amount in excess of the $1,000 billion it already owes, and not paying it back currently. The money market, therefore, has the competence to handle at least $65 billion of the funding the new venture requires *assuming that as the purchase price is paid to the government, it uses those funds to pay out present debts.* To ensure that this does happen, the purchase price for the project as raised could be deposited in a trust to which government bond and bill holders would bring bonds and bills for redemption. In effect, the government would receive no cash in so far as its purchase price is concerned but it would be freed from the liability for bonds and bills on a dollar for dollar basis. Conversely, the new project, in raising the purchase price of $75 billion, would incur liabilities in that amount. It would also receive no cash. If that transfer could be effected the new project would have issued enough shares of stock to transfer $75 billion of government debt into equity in the project and incurred liabilities of $75 billion for the purchase price. In addition, it would have to raise a further $25 billion to be able to operate. The liabilities of the new company, therefore, would be—

Debt
    $ 75 billion for the purchase price

Capital Account
    $ 75 billion equity issue to cancel government liabilities
    $ 25 billion equity issue for operations
    $175 billion

Its assets would be—
    $ 25 billion cash proceeds for operation
    $150 billion in assets purchased from the government
    $175 billion

Thus the new project has in effect paid $150 billion for the government assets it has acquired.

Its debt structure ratio is—

$25 billion cash ÷ $75 billion for the purchase price which equals .33. Although it is solvent in terms of its debt structure ratio, it is not sufficiently solvent that the private banks want its business since we know the ratio of .50 is the lower end of that desire. It is true that many new projects, in fact most new projects, start out with debt structure ratios that low and lower. We are not talking about just any new business, however, but *the largest business in the history of the world.*

Furthermore, although it is solvent in terms of its debt structure ratio, it is not solvent in terms of its ownership structure ratio. That is, it can never pay out its owners. We can see this by applying principles we have used previously in calculating government net worth. On that basis, its net worth is

$$7.1 \times (25+75) \times (.0223) = \$15.83 \text{ billion.}$$

With generated savings of only $2.23 billion its calculated net worth plus generated savings is only $15.83 plus 2.23 equals $18.06 billion. Implicitly, its market value is $100 billion dollars since its equity was sold at that value. The ratio of its $N+E_t$ to its market value, what we have called its "ownership structure ratio", is $18.06/100 = .18$. Although it is solvent in terms of the viability of receivables working out payables, *it is insolvent in terms of paying out its owners.*

There must be a better compromise. Either current bond holders must accept less than dollar for dollar equity for debt in return for certain voting privileges, or those buying the equity for operations must pay more for certain privileges. In actual fact, to bring the ownership structure ratio up to .33, the level of the debt structure ratio, one way or another equity holders must be prepared to accept about 54¢ for every dollar they put in. Although this is a vast amount of "water" to have out front in any project, especially in the world's largest, I believe that it is possible to convince fund managers to be long-sighted enough to accept it. Let us consider this claim now that our science has given us some of the important scale factors.

Currently, government debt is the major investment available for fund managers. If the thesis is accepted that it is governmental insolvency that is causing the remarkable rise in interest rates and if the thesis is accepted that buying government assets is the cure for that insolvency, then we can estimate the cost to fund managers of *not* accepting the required water. That cost is clearly the rapid decline of the market value of portfolios of government debt that reflects the rise in the rate of interest, a decline that must accelerate if fund managers do not take the necessary steps to bail government out. Consider the following example. One dollar invested in government bills or bonds for one year at 10% has a present value of 90.91¢. The present value of that $1 as the rate of interest rises for debts of one and two year periods is as of the following table:

Rate of Interest %	P V of $1 (1 year)	P V of $1 (2 years)
10	90.91¢	82.64¢
11	90.09	81.16
12	89.28	79.72
13	88.49	78.31
14	87.72	76.95
15	86.95	75.61
16	86.21	74.32
17	85.47	73.05
18	84.74	71.82
19	84.03	70.62
20	83.33	69.44
21	82.64	68.30
22	81.97	67.19
23	81.30	66.10
24	80.64	65.03
25	80.00	64.00

Thus, if shortly after the fund manager purchases government debt for one year at 15% the rate offered for new government debt of one year increases to 16%, for each dollar's worth the fund manager holds he has lost 86.95 − 86.21 = .74¢. If he holds $50 million of it, his loss in present value is $370,000. If he holds $50 million of two year debt, on the other hand, his loss in present value is 75.61 − 74.32 = 1.29¢ for every dollar. His loss is $645,000. That is, if he sells the paper he holds when the new and higher rate prevails he will obtain not $100 million for it but

	$100 million	
less	.370	
less	.645	
	$ 98.985	million

Thinking of the whole United States debt of $1,000 billion, and assuming 50% is held by fund managers in the form of one-and two-year paper, the result of an increase in the interest rate of 1% from 15% to 16% is a loss of present value to those funds of .00989 × 500 = $4.94 billion. If we think of such rate increases happening three times a year, the total loss per year is running at about $15 billion.

Although there is nothing rigorous about these calculations, they cannot be far from the truth. In five years, therefore, governmental insolvency which is causing the persistent rise in interest rates will cost fund managers about $75 billion. For them to accept water of roughly half that amount in the new project and to give up debt and replace it with equity in so doing is not a bad deal. For them to do so, they need near-certainty that interest rate increases will cease. In so far as interest rates do decrease they stand to gain with the debt they still hold.

Thus I believe strong arguments can be made to fund managers that they should bear the brunt of the water in the new project. Their rapidly mounting losses in present value of all debt will be cut back. If the new project is sufficiently massive that it does return government to solvency, not only will those losses decrease but, in so far as the interest rate is decreased, the losses will be turned into profits.

In fact those results are so predictable that it should be possible to state clearly how much water fund managers are accepting in the project by taking equity in it and what the interest rate scenario is that gives them better than dollar for dollar for it. Making this quantitative demonstration is one of the major responsibilities of Objective Economics.

Aside from the attitudes fund managers and investors may have toward switching government debt to equity in the new project, they must be conscious of the repercussions of an underwriting sold in public markets for proceeds of at least $25 billion. Most fund managers and other large investors hold substantial portfolios of equity as well as debt. Further, the total net sale of new equities in the United

States, i.e. net of retirements of equities, is estimated by various authorities for 1981 at between $20 and $25 billion. Thus the new project alone would equate all other net equity issues for the year. Unquestionably an offering that massive in the United States markets could and probably would drive the whole stock market down dramatically as other equities were sold to buy it.

I think the answer to this problem has to rest with the resolution made of two others. One is the admissibility of foreign buying of the stock, particularly by the governments that have extremely high debt structure ratios such as OPEC governments and that of Alberta. The other is the welcome the equity offering could be given in other major stock exchanges, particularly those of London, Tokyo, Paris, Toronto and Amsterdam.

The former of these questions, that of foreign ownership, must needs arise in any case because it probably is not possible to make a clearcut distinction between civil and military space technology. Military aspects of space technology probably already involve foreign links and even some ownership. Surely it is conceivable that terms can be negotiated that would satisfy both foreign investors, governmental and private, and the United States Government that would be selling the bulk of the assets into the new project. Without doubt, some secrecy, real or imagined, would be lost and some foreign buyers, if allowed to buy too much, could pose major problems as to priorities within the commercialization of the know-how. Certain covenants would undoubtedly be necessary and some voting board representation by foreign groups would be required. Perhaps even the United Nations would have to be represented on the board, but without a vote, just to allay any suspicion of foreign governments that were unable to participate directly as owners. All such accommodations are complicated to conceive and there is little point in our speculating about them. The basic problem is to stop inflation. If conviction grows that it can be stopped by this means we can expect at least a favorable climate for the necessary accommodations.

The use that can be made of foreign stock exchanges really depends upon the same conviction. No country with a major stock exchange can see inflation as anything but worrisome. If all can be convinced that sale of government assets is the correct approach to getting rid of inflation and if space technology can be packaged as a commercial venture that captures everyone's imagination, there is every reason to expect a welcome for the equity offering all over the world. The more exchanges contribute to it the less damage, however short-lived, it will do to equities currently on those markets.

A great deal depends upon the two principles guiding us: the one that we are at last dealing with inflation in a manner that will work; and the other that space technology can capture our imagination to the degree required. Most of this book has dealt with the first principle. Let us examine the second principle in slightly more detail than I have evoked previously.

The space programs of the USA and the Soviet Union have been without question the most dramatic pulling together of science and engineering arts in the history of man. Their scope in terms of subject matter has ranged over every field of physical science from physics to genetics, i.e. from non-life to life sciences. The engineering problems have ranged from human nutrition to containment materials that often have had to encompass incredible ranges of stress, flexibility, temperature and radiation. In all of these cases not only have workable solutions been devised but without doubt thousands of alternative solutions that narrowly missed acceptance are recorded, many of them suggestive of other opportunities and applications.

To me, pulling all these know-hows together into a commercial package is making virtually the whole of human knowledge including much of its speculation into a supermarket. Inevitably the new company will become the mother lode that feeds almost every research establishment in the world, no matter what the specialty involved. Its business will of necessity be invention and innovation, and its customers will be the innovators.

I suspect it is correct to say that an organization such as NASA has drawn on the resources of other research and development establishments such as Bell Laboratories more than it has drawn on its own. Inevitably the new company will reverse that flow. Inevitably, in doing so, the nature of such single groups will be changed drastically. In fact many will be pulled right into the new company and direct contractual links will be forged with present parent companies.

One gain to society that I see in this is a greater opportunity for theoretical work to be conducted in all fields of enquiry. Good as the present research and development establishment is, the very fact that it tends to be project oriented, because of the relatively narrow parameters of development in individual companies, reveals that theoretical research without specific project focus is often impossible to fund. This is unfortunate because our great gains in instrumentality follow most economically from theory, not practice. Further, theoretical research is vastly cheaper to conduct than is project oriented research. We cannot place too fine a point on this issue but I expect that the major pulling together of space technology that I envisage in the new company could lead to gains in our theoretical understanding as we enter into the 21st century that are comparable to those with which we entered the 20th.

It is for these reasons that I find it very difficult to conceive the new company divorced from the educational system, at least in its higher levels. The negative side of this from the point of view of the university establishment is that most corporations that currently support universities financially would rather see their funds spent as investments in the new company. The positive side from my point of view is that they probably would be correct. That there are major problems in the university system all over the western world is palpable. Perhaps it is time that it met competition from an organization that ultimately must survive in the market place. Whether or not this is so it is highly probable that pulling together the know-how we are envisaging will relieve governments of substantial funding inputs to the system of higher education.

Perhaps the most important of all considerations, however, is the contribution the new company can make to world peace. The very scale of the government sell-out that is required for governmental solvency will imply that the new company is born internationally. The very fact that there is no sharp dividing line between civil and military know-how will bring into that international delivery room a careful scrutiny of the trade-off between secrecy and surveillance. I believe that any such scrutiny made under the urgent necessity of getting rid of inflation must find on the side of surveillance and against secrecy. I can see all governments of the world contributing substantial fees to our company to maintain world-wide surveillance of all dangers to mankind be they natural in origin or products of our technical skills.

It is perhaps interesting to point out that governments have not done particularly well in looking after such problems on behalf of people. Perhaps protecting mankind from those problems would be better handled by a corporation with wide international involvements in terms of staff and ownership but that incidentally pays its way and pays out its owners. We tend to forget in this modern world of big government and nationalist slogans that many, perhaps most, of the spectacular rises of peoples, the rise of Florence and other Italian cities, the rise of German principalities, indeed, most such events up to the Napoleonic Wars and later, involved heavy reliance upon companies in the business of war. Frequently those events led to major results with remarkably small loss of life. In fact on some occasions the "people" found themselves much more as spectators at a sporting event than as victims of war. If we do merge know-how as I am envisaging, just how necessary are large armies, large air forces, large navies? Is it possible that instead of commercial considerations leading us to war as many allege has been and is the case, that the real problem is that we have stopped commercializing war?

I realize these are dangerous waters, for many do dearly love to wave flags and many more see virtue in the national aggressive state that honors its war dead. Having sampled both trade and war, however, I hold a strong preference for the former. You can get killed at the latter. In any case, if the chairman of our new company wished to propose that, for a fee, his company would look after wars for us, I should be prone to reading the proposal.

The burden of these comments is that if once we fix our minds on the enormous pooling of know-how I am foreseeing, our imaginations run wild. The whole of world society can tingle with the vibrations of a process of discovery that emanates from people brought together not on the basis of race, color, sex, religion and all the other nonsenses of life, but on the basis of intellect. Once in a while we get a glimpse of this excitement: the break in Walter Cronkite's voice when the first man steps on the moon; the awe at the first landing of the space shuttle. These are great moments that suddenly make us walk erect. Are we depriving ourselves of many of those moments? Is that deprivation one of the costs of inflation? I think it is.

I propose to leave our new company wherever I have located it in your imagination. There are some other aspects of passive resistance to insolvent governments that I must discuss. Obviously we cannot count on one single scheme to do the job of getting rid of inflation for us. Although nothing else of similar effectiveness appears to exist, there are some less exciting things we can do that will help. I now examine them.

CHAPTER 25

Identifying Insolvent Government as the Enemy

(a) *Suborning the "Commons"*

The reader has undoubtedly grasped much of what has happened to society in the last 50 years that made it fertile territory for inflation. Instead of government carrying out its function of governing and leaving its encroachments on the economy to what private banking would and would not yield, it thrust itself upon the economy by subverting those natural disciplines.

I hope not to be misunderstood in this. Private banking is itself a subversion of natural disciplines of economic activity. The rise of banking cannot be distinguished from the rise of mankind from the single marauding individual into a society of individuals that was gathered progressively into local or "city" states, then into national states and finally into internationalism. At every juncture in this "progress" some form of annihilating obligations had to be found that made possible both the expansion into the larger domain and the limitation of that expansion which yielded the generation of savings. Just as our minds cannot conceive expansion without limit, so does nature abhor it. The generation of savings reflects that abhorrence.

Thus, even central banks which began in the 16th and 17th centuries in Italy and England are and have been part of the rise of mankind. They represent for a highly developed stage of national states what Lombardy bankers represented for an earlier stage of city states and small principalities. They have performed the function of slowing down the action, as much happened behind their protective shield that generated savings. In the simplest terms, they have played their role of making sure that all the chickens do not always come home to roost at the same time—that the economy never "pays itself out" so to speak, making a particular "now" both the end and the beginning.

At every stage in this controlled explosion and implosion beginning with our earlier ancestors the danger has existed that the process would happen too fast. The defence against this has always been the Old Order the New Order is replacing. There is nothing either good or bad about the private banking discipline except this: relative to central banking, it is an Old Order that, in being replaced by the New, makes sure that it keeps the New within bounds. Objective Economics has found what those bounds are. Modern government through its central bank has clearly leaped over them, subverting the disciplines of the Old Order so violently that inflation has resulted.

The people or, more specifically, the "Commons", have nearly always been part of the Old Order limiting the aggression of the New Order as represented by the Executive. Historically they have played a watchdog role to limit the executive branch of government in its almost continuous flirtation with insolvency. Back to King John of Magna Carta fame, back to the Caesars, back to Alexander of Macedon, the proneness of those who led government to lead it to insolvency, to suborn and subvert the solvency disciplines inherent in natural economic law too quickly is a fact that cries at us from every page of history. Virtually the whole of Aristotle's essay on Economics (as distinct from his essay on Politics) is devoted to a recounting of various schemes of leaders of government up to his time by which disciplines of the system were subverted more violently and more quickly than the Commons willingly allowed. It is indeed possible to read the whole of history as this evolutionary process that continually brings the precocious executive branch of government to the heel of the Commons as the Commons itself moves forward to become a

New Order. The contest of New and Old has rarely been equal. Sometimes great leaps forward or backward have resulted and sometimes long periods of stagnation have existed. Only of this are we certain: if bounds are exceeded, nature exacts enormous retribution.

What is perhaps unique about the precociousness of the Executive in this century that has broken those bounds is the intellectual content of the rationale for its action, action that has created inflation. Henry VIII had little intellectual rationale for his inauguration of the international hegemony of England and the accompanying bankrupting of the Treasury of his father. Louis XIV had even less for the extravagance of Versailles and the War of the Spanish Succession. The Executive of modern states, however, from the publication of Keynes' *General Theory* in the mid 1930's, has rationalized its encroachment on the economy with ever deeper plunges into intellectuality—not *evidence* that it was required, but *intellectuality*. Like the proponents of a "rational religion", that Executive has first convinced itself and then, in methods little short of brain-washing, convinced its Commons that such encroachments were necessary, just, and right, to protect the Commons from itself. Keynes is directly responsible for this outrage, an outrage that has led the Commons to accept guilt for creating inflation.

It is absolutely fundamental to curing inflation that all of us except the Executive free ourselves from this guilt. Even if we do force the sell-out cure of the previous discussion upon government, unless we take steps to understand that causing inflation does not lie within the competence of the millions of small to large entities within the economy to create, it will simply recur. Inflation is the prerogative of the very large entity that can bring into the economy a mechanism for annihilating obligations that can subvert the rules of the Old Order. Only central governments have that competence and therefore it is nigh universally true that they, not the people, not the Commons, have caused inflation and continue to do so.

(b) *Freeing Ourselves from Keynesian Guilt*

Although most people have never read Keynes' work of the 1930's, certain of his allegations have become part of the national and international consciousness. A central theme dominates all others that we might have taken from his work: unless government intervenes actively in the economy, the economy will perform in less than an ideal manner in its service to mankind. Specifically, Keynes argued (as distinct from demonstrated scientifically) that there was no reason to expect the economy to tend toward ideal circumstances such as full employment, minimum prices or maximum output. Economists prior to Keynes, implicitly or explicitly had seen economic activity as heading always in these directions and had in general warned against interference lest that progress be hindered. Keynes argued that sufficient reasons did not exist for seeing the best of all worlds as the inevitable outcome of economic activity and unless we, that is government, interfered, there were any number of less than optimal points at which the economy would aim. Thus was born the rationale, an intellectual rather than a demonstrable rationale, for governmental encroachment on the economy.

In his day, Keynes emphasized the facts of unemployment and low or falling prices since they were the most glaring economic problems. Shorn of many important details of a complicated argument, he concluded that without substantial initiatives by government to increase spending in the economy, it could and had become "stuck", as it were, at a level of employment that fell far short of ideal and that low prices were one of the problems associated with it. When we translate that argument to a domain of facts in which the problems seem to be that prices are rising too fast and although *un*employment is higher than desired, *em*ployment is very high, it seems to follow that we are spending too much. In the 1930's case, we seemed to be spending too little and government had to step in to bring our spending up. In the 1970's and 1980's we seem to be spending too much and both the government and we must cut back.

I venture to say that nearly everybody is prepared to accept that claim. It has become part of our mother wit as it were. Few politicians have omitted it from their speeches in the past decade. Few board chairmen have omitted it from their annual reports. Most writers about the economy make direct or indirect reference to it. It has become the hair shirt of modern society—we spend too much of our income and save too little.

We know, that is, readers of this book do, that the issue has never been how much or how little people or even governments spend as a portion of their income. We know that the issue has never been how much or how little they save as a portion of their income. We also know that the issue has never been how much or how little they invest as a portion of their income. The issue is and always has been, *how much they are owed as a ratio of how much they owe,* i.e. their individual debt structure ratios, and *also the ratio of the sum of their net worth and generated savings to their market value*, i.e. their ownership structure ratios. Both high and low values of these ratios cause inflation if the entities involved are large enough or if many smaller entities cluster in these regions. In other words, *both* forms of insolvency cause major inefficiencies in the use of money in the economy, inefficiencies in the use of goods in the economy, and inefficiencies in the pull of the one or the other, which is to say, leverage. Deflation, on the other hand, is an *ever-present* tendency of economies that manifests itself by the tendency for low ratios to be pulled up and high ratios to be pulled down as the economy ever seeks maximum efficiency. Deflation is the *natural* tendency of all economies, its free gift or "invisible hand", whereas inflation requires that man work against that tendency.

Thus, inflation and deflation, when viewed in terms of efficiency with which economies work, are not symmetrically opposite processes. Left to their own devices economies deflate to maximum efficiency. That is what the law of constrained fall to states of least economic energy is all about. By contrast, what stops economies from inflating unless truly extraordinary efforts are made is the activity of the private banking systems that I have described as "polarization". As the ratios of some entities fall excessively, banks, at certain values of these ratios become restrictive to the customers that manifest them, and the reverse to their imaginary counter-entity. As the ratios of some entites rise, banks become restrictive to their imaginary counter-entity and the reverse to those real entities. The result is a tendency to "balance", albeit a jiggly sort of balance because that balance tends not to be around a single pivot point, but around three: *least* generated savings (money used most efficiently); least investment (goods used most efficiently); [79] and most leverage (the pull of money on goods and goods on money at maximum efficiency). Because of the pull of these three extrema, even slight shocks to the economy lead to movements away from maximum efficiency. Thus, although *de*flation is the economy's tendency, it also tends to reveal a smaller but fairly steady tendency to *in*flate away from its deflated state. In short, the so-called "secular price rise" over long periods of time that history has manifested is itself the result of minor shocks that were probably short-lived.

The doctrine that the cause of inflation is the high spending habits of people thus falls to the ground when we take into account the modalities of banking behavior. Banks are led to discouraging the availability of credit to people who spend themselves into insolvency, and encouraging its availability to people who use little or none. Recently this "blame the consumer" irrelevancy has been described as "inflationary expectations". In this thesis, people are alleged to spend and take on new credit commitments on the basis of their expectation of inflation. Thus, if I buy a house expecting its market value to go up 5% per year because of inflation and assume a mortgage of 17.5%, I am alleged to view that rate of interest as only 17.5% − 5% = 12.5%. Thus I shall be about as willing to assume that mortgage as I should have been if I had no inflation expectation and the rate were 12.5%. In effect, therefore, instead of a 17.5% mortgage rate discouraging me from spending, perhaps a rate of 20% would be required to do so, which is to say, 17.5% actually encourages me to spend. People, that is all the you's and me's, are still seen as "fueling inflation" because of these inflationary expectations.

This argument, that places the blame for inflation on people, reverses cause and effect. If inflation means *in fact*, not in prospect, that my chequing flows reveal to the banks that I am a customer with whom they wish to do business then they will certainly encourage me to borrow and spend the limit. If I exceed the limit, if despite inflation my account starts to reveal chequing flows of a ratio of .50 or lower, I shall soon find my spending binge is brought to an end. Only if I can conceal the facts from the banks, which in general means that only if I am represented by a central bank that can "suck the banks in" as it were, by annihilating obligations, can I go beyond that point. My inflationary expectations might well have led me to proposition my banker. His might well have led him to proposition me. In the cold light of dawn, however, it is my chequing flow that determines whether we have a repeat engagement or whether I go my way and he goes his.

The essential point is that inflation cannot be hung on psychology whatever that word is supposed to mean. That is so because the laws of economic activity as demonstrated in Chapter 2 are not psychological but natural. People as people, as distinct from people as actors, simply have nothing to do with them. The means and ends of people, their expectations, their dreams, hopes and despairs mean nothing in the great sweep of the natural laws of economic activity.

Given that no entities in the economy, except those struggling into existence and perhaps some that are dying off, have insolvent debt and ownership structure ratios, money, goods and the pull of the one on the other always tend to operate close to maximum efficiency. This is true whether the level of spending is very high or very low. As long as government remains solvent, it is perfectly proper for it to raise or lower its spending and in so doing increase activity levels or decrease them provided it does so extremely carefully. Since inflation is the difference between the sum of net worth and generated savings of the banks and their market value, the government must act upon both quantities in such a manner as not to change that difference significantly. On the other hand its action must not change the ratio of the two quantities significantly since $(N+E_t) \div V$ of the banks is their ownership structure ratio. Further, whatever the amount of inflation or deflation in the economy when the government acts, if its action changes the ratio of that amount to the amount of the currency issue, its action will either depreciate or appreciate the currency, which is to say, increase or decrease the number of people to whom each dollar bill is implicitly promised.

It is only in the conservation range for all major entities in the economy, including both government and banks, in which these three contradictory guidelines of government action cause little problem. It therefore follows that if the economy is operating close to maximum efficiency, which is to say, all major entities including the government have solvent debt and ownership structure ratios, that there is some running room for government encroachment. If, however, a major entity such as government itself is not distinctly solvent in either or both senses then encroachment will lead to decreases in efficiency whatever activity levels (i.e. whatever levels of R, P, N, E_t, and V) those encroachments achieve. It is these decreases in efficiency that yield us confusing pictures of *rising* prices, *falling* currencies, rising *em*ployment and rising *un*employment.

Thus we have ample grounds to question the truth of both propositions that government *should* encroach on the economy and that our spending or even that of the government are crucial considerations. Our *solvency* and that of the government are crucial. In not having a science of solvency, Keynes and his successors such as Friedman, the father of modern "monetarism", simply ignored that fact.

The scientific truth is that economies neither deflate nor inflate unless one or the other or both of our two ratios change. Further, without the convenience of a central bank to subvert the banking discipline for us, it is virtually impossible for us, no matter who we are, to change those ratios into levels that cause inflation. In short, the only spender whose spending causes inflation is the central government for whom the central bank works. And such spending results from governmental insolvency that it can achieve and has achieved because it has a central bank that we do not have.

Let us therefore cleanse our consciences once and for all of any guilt for inflation. We have nothing to do with causing it simply because our banks will not let us. Some of us gain by it and some of us lose but none of us, even Massey Ferguson or Chrysler, causes it. [80] The continued allegation by government leaders that inflation is a people-caused thing is not only a lie; it should qualify as a slander or libel under the law of the land. A test case in the courts against the Prime Minister of Canada, who is much given to asserting that people cause inflation, might achieve much to stop this vicious abrogation of responsibility. For the governors or chairmen of our central banks to make such allegations is even more serious because they are in fact the agents directly responsible for creating enough inflation to allow their governmental clients continued access to the economy.[81] Whether legal action against them is likely to succeed or not is questionable because they are agents and not principals— at least that is the advice I have had from counsel.

The use of the law to make inflation-creation more and more difficult for government is a relatively unexplored channel and one I hope many individuals and organizations will examine carefully. Proposition 13 in California used the vote to achieve similar ends and most governments operate under borrowing authority that must be renewed periodically by the Commons. In Ottawa and in Washington renewing and increasing that latter authority has run into more and more opposition within government itself. Use of referenda such as Proposition 13 and statutory borrowing authority, however, are not nearly as useful as use of the courts. One of the advantages of the courts is that in most administrations if a prima facie case of strength can be made, injunctions that stop the alleged activity at issue can sometimes be obtained. This is rather like a two by four plank across the bridge of the nose for governments that usually have many ways of delaying action if injunctions are not threatened. An injunction to stop the Bank of Canada or the United States Treasury from bringing unregistered paper to market would elicit something between a 10- and 20-second delay before the battle was joined. An injunction to stop a government with an insolvent debt structure ratio from taking any action which lowered that ratio would perhaps require a further ten seconds before the battle was joined. I do not need to elaborate these statements.

CHAPTER 26

Rules of Conduct for Inflation-Fighting Societies

Guilt for causing inflation should certainly be felt. It should be felt by the right institution, however, namely insolvent government. A whole new pattern of attitudes to government needs to be developed to ensure that guilt rests there and is not shifted. I list some of the details of those attitudes:

(1) Feel free to view the central government as society's enemy, and resent motherhood statements that you should feel otherwise.

(2) Since your central government is likely insolvent and hence causing inflation, treat its agents and representatives *as* insolvents. Be extremely cautious in using them as agents to pay your bills. If you owe them money and they owe you money, always send the net amount or an invoice; never send them money if you can legally avoid doing so.

(3) Do not pay much attention to government pronouncements except on law and order or peace and war. The statements of intent and the explanations of insolvents are more or less

meaningless; if meaningful, they are calculated misrepresentations. In particular do not give the media evidence that you are interested in government and whenever possible inform them you are not. The economics of newsgathering from government are so favorable that given half a chance the media would report nothing but government news. Indeed, some media are almost guilty of that now.

(4) Do not lend the government money any more easily than you would lend an insolvent neighbor money. If you currently hold government debt, sell it as soon as you can find a satisfactory replacement. If you have influence with institutions in the money market make it known to them that you do not want them to lend to or borrow from government. Sell stocks you may own in companies that lend to or borrow from government extensively.

(5) Disabuse your mind of all thoughts that supporting insolvent government financially, specifically by lending to it, is patriotic. It is not. By doing so you hurt your fellow man if not yourself. Disabuse your mind also of all willingness to believe that government-backed debt is secure as a matter of course, or because, as the Bank of Canada has had the effrontery to say in some of its advertisements, it is "backed by the resources of Canada." The central government has a set of books and all entities in the economy including yourself have as well. Those books tell us whose resources are whose. Such a statement by the Bank of Canada is an assertion of powers of expropriation neither it nor its government has or could obtain without the most violent debate.

(6) To the best of your ability do not allow any business entity you control to seek or take advantage of government grants of any kind. If your entity is in the charity business and thus is virtually dependent on government, make every effort to replace government funding by funding from private sources.

(7) If you play the inflation expectations game in your own life with or without encouragement from government, do not let

it blind you to the reality of your chequing flow. All such play presumes a sale of an acquired asset sometime in the future. Make sure you do sell to keep the juices flowing in your bank account or the bank will end the game when you least expect it.

(8) Do not become caught up in slogans such as "cutting expenditures", "balancing the budget", "there is no free lunch", "moderate demands for wages", "spend less, save more, and work harder", etc. Insolvent government has only the option of insolvents which is basically to sell assets. All these slogans either detract from a clear vision of that option and its necessity or blame you for the actions of government. There is nothing wrong with you that is any of the government's business. The wrong is with government.

(9) Learn to yawn if you do not already do so when central bankers explain what they allege to be the facts of life. Never let the thought out of your mind that their sole function is to make sure today and every day that there is enough inflation in the economy to allow their government to meet its obligations.

(10) With civility, kindness, but the firmest of conviction, be uncooperative with all but law and good order that emanates from government. The passive resistance of Mahatma Ghandi freed India. Your passive resistance can free your government from its insolvency.

Footnotes

[1] Dimensionless Science Publications Limited, 1979, by the author.

[2] Published by Harvard University Press, 1971.

[3] Another, of great significance for the future, is its potential for predicting the stock market. That potential ensures a compelling interest in Objective Economics for the trading connection of government. It will serve us subsequently in this book in our exposure of the fundamental scientific shortcomings of the subjective economics.

[4] This is of course a vast oversimplification. As Deutscher explains in his classic biography of Stalin, even before Lenin's first illness, Stalin had control of the administrative reins.

[5] The data available allowed us only 273 usable companies.

[6] *Freedom and Reform* by Frank H. Knight, Harper & Brothers, 1947, p.14. This is a reference to Knight's paper, "Freedom as Fact and Criterion", a title that has influenced the title of my chapter.

[7] P.D. Ouspensky has been on my conscience for some years ever since a colleague (Mr. Pat Michalak) called my attention to similar thought trends to his in Objective Economics. Now, my editor has made the same reminder. Accordingly I quote Ouspensky at some length, as follows: "But in the activities of his life, particularly with activities of the kind that many people are concerned in and when years pass between the beginning of something and its result, a man can very easily deceive himself and take the result 'obtained' as the result desired, that is, believe that he has won when on the whole he has lost...."

"The greatest insult for a 'man-machine' is to tell him that he can do nothing, can attain nothing, that he can never move towards any aim whatever and that in striving towards one he will inevitably create another. Actually of course it cannot be otherwise. The 'man-machine' is in the power of accident. His activities may fall by accident into some sort of channel which has been created by cosmic or mechanical forces and they may by accident move along this channel for a certain time, giving the illusion that aims of some kind are being attained. Such accidental correspondence of results with the aims we have set before us or the attainment of aims in small things which can have no consequences creates in mechanical man the conviction that he is able to attain any aim, 'is able to conquer nature' as it is called, is able to 'arrange the whole of his life', and so on."

In Search of the Miraculous, Harcourt Brace, 1949, p.133.

[8] Knight, op. cit., p. 12.

[9] Adopting a stable terminology for the three concepts, generated savings, investment, and leverage, has been a difficult problem. In *How ALL Economies Work* I called what I now call generated savings, "ability to meet obligations" and what I now call investment, the "dollars required to retain

economic state''. Prof. Warren Blackman, with a great flash of insight, grasped that what I was calling ability to meet obligations was really objectively generated savings. That insight allowed me to identify dollars required to retain economic state as investment and as a *retardation* of generated savings. Leverage is the only one of these three basic quantities that has retained its original title. Prof. David Cape, however, has helped me clarify what it is.

[10] Investment, different from both generated savings and leverage, depends only upon the debt structure ratio, i.e. R/P, and not upon $R + P$. Thus, to identify savings and investment (as Keynes does) *requires* a factor or proportionality because they are dimensionally different. Keynes made his identity a tautology by defining ''money'' ab initio, and viewing savings as part of it. He then assumed the factor of proportionality was unity, by conceiving investment not as a *degree of retardation* of savings but as all savings dropping down a well.

[11] I owe the term ''constrained'' to Prof. Cape who pointed out to me that since there are three *targets* of the fall, a fall to any one is constrained by the other two.

[12] The parallel with the experience of physics is worth taking a step farther. Once we realize that the economic barriers that have been violated to create inflation are ranges of debt structure ratios over which ''conservation principles'' hold, we cannot help but remind ourselves that a major threat to a physical conservation principle (conservation of energy) lies right at the heart of physical theory leading up to, and that was required for, the realization of fission. In the literature of physics, Dirac caused the problem because when he made wave mechanics Lorentz covariant, and solved major problems in doing so, he created the possibility of a negative kinetic energy state.

Rather than accepting the implied violation of the conservation of energy and redesigning physics on a dimensionless basis free of an isotropy assumption, and free of Daltonian particles, a positively charged ''electron'' was postulated. Later called the positron, and ''discovered'' at least by inference, this particle was built in to a theory of its ''annihilation'' by the electron. This theory was absolutely fundamental to Fermi's success in the Manhattan Project which was the first controlled fission experiment, and which finally yielded the atomic bomb.

It is interesting to note that very few years later in a totally unrelated sequence of events, Graham Towers, the first Governor of the Bank of Canada, successfully negotiated the Purchase and Resale Agreement with designated brokers making the bank their lender of last recourse. This agreement created an ''obligation-annihilation'' mechanism that was desperately needed if his central bank was to *be* a bank in a Canadian system in which private banks used the New York market (customers' acceptances and letters of credit) as their way of annihilating obligations. American banks, by comparison, for many years prior to 1915 when the Federal Reserve Board was set up, had used a central banker's rediscount rate as the vehicle of annihilating obligations. As we shall see later, annihilation of obligations is a principal component of the method whereby banks create their extremely high ratios of generated savings to net worth.

In point of history, it is likely true that as a result of the Bank of England's involvement in the South Sea Bubble, that event came very close to being the first "atomic explosion". Only by "fusing" government equity in the South Sea project with the Bank of England's net worth, was Walpole, the Prime Minister of the day, able to hold the bank together. In view of these events it is interesting to remind ourselves that the great physicist, Sir Isaac Newton, was one of the designers of the Bank of England.

13 All evidence in physics of particles is inferential. In cloud chamber work, for example, we see "paths of particles", never particles.

14 As in the physical domain, this annihilation happens extremely quickly, so quickly in fact, that economic literature has never related the process to how banks work to develop the credit structure. That literature retains to this day the fiction that that structure results from banks borrowing, keeping a reserve of some percentage, lending the remainder, etc., despite the fact that no one ever saw a bank "keep" a reserve as distinct from rustling around trying to beg, borrow, or steal what the central bank mandates on a particular day.

15 It is because these conservation ranges exist and because neither Keynes nor Friedman had a theory of insolvency to apply outside those ranges, that each of those authors makes a kind of sense in basing their theories on certain alleged stable relations. Keynes hinged his theory on an alleged stable relation between savings and investment and such does exist in their overlapped conservation ranges. Friedman hinged his theory on an alleged stable relation between the "demand for money" (read "leverage" in our terms) and investment. Such does exist in their overlapped conservation ranges. For neither case, however, does such a stable relation exist when the entity's debt structure ratio lies outside the conservation ranges. See my technical note "Getting Keynesianism and Friedmanism in Focus", Progress Report 1980 of the Institute of Objective Economics.

16 Net worth can be read out of the balance sheet. Essentially it is original funds put in by owners, plus undistributed or "retained earnings". New equity funds entering must also be added in.

17 As stated previously, this expression refers to tendencies to the *minima* of investment and generated savings, and to the *maximum* of leverage. Since the debt structure ratios of these three extrema all differ somewhat, the "state of least economic energy" contains non-singularity or, in Marxist terms, "contradiction". It is dynamic rather than static. It can be shown that one of the results of this is a permanent, long term tendency to price rise (i.e. "secular price rise").

18 In more advanced applications of Objective Economics we are able to use this concept to give us a definition of *economic work* as deduced from the dynamics of the balance sheet. Investment increase introduces an interplay of net worth in the balance sheet with other parts of it. Once economic work is discovered, it is but a short step to recognize in the balance sheet processes that are none other than transformations of our three types of economic energy, generated savings, investment, and leverage.

[19] Persistent near unity debt structure ratios are not a sufficient definition of a "bank". Two other conditions are accumulated depreciation per dollar of receivables that approaches zero, and annihilation of obligations that bears a ratio with payables that "waxes" and "wanes" but appears to increase secularly (see note 17 above). Somewhat colloquially, a bank is an entity that borrows money, takes a quick look over its shoulder to see if there is a borrower available, and if there is not, it annihilates the obligation.

[20] The Greek philosopher, Aristotle, (circa 350 BC) in his Politics, Book I, Ch. X, argued against interest payments on the grounds that money, i.e. the coin of the realm, different from living things, could not breed. Money was not, in short, in a state of "becoming". In Objective Economics, the barrenness of money is incorporated in the form of an assumed equal and opposite property of discounting and accumulation. The reason it is thus incorporated is not, however, because we play philosopher. It is basic that we not take the existence of *any* rate of interest for granted. This we avoid by assumption (b) above.

[21] The literature actually contains a middle ground between the statistical laws of the German historical school and the laws of Objective Economics. This is what is called "Pareto's Law". Thanks to a recent article by D. Sahal, "Formulation of the Pareto Distribution", Environment and Planning A, 1978 Vol. 10, pages 1363-1376, we can see Pareto's Law as a consequence of "dimensional homogeneity" suggestive of "generative processes from within". Objective Economics, by comparison, is a "dimensionless science" that, in essence, denies dimensional homogeneity on the grounds that we cannot assert, for an observed system of activity, that "any number is or is not a member of a given set of numbers." It appears to follow that if we cannot make that assertion, which underlies both the Weierstrass theorem of the limit and Dedekind's theory of real number continuity, *we can never separate what we measure from what we measure it with.* The problem of all science is learning to live with that fact. I am grateful to Mr. Burke Brown, President of Merchant Bancorp, for copying me with the Sahal article.

[22] The *General Theory of Interest and Employment* by John Maynard Keynes was first published in 1936. That theory used macroeconomic aggregates that were given what logical basis they can be given in his earlier book, *Treatise on Money.*

[23] That is, we must discard such concepts as aggregated note issues plus demand deposits, or the various money aggregates reported by banking systems. All such concepts are ab initio definitions of money whereas it is the on-going function of economic activity to create the abstraction that "money" must be, if the past and future are to be consistent with "now".

[24] What its bank is doing is lending *by* borrowing, and borrowing *by* lending. Empty bank accounts and empty loan accounts are a constant threat to these modalities. The bank is also annihilating obligations it has acquired by borrowing—and that it cannot get rid of by lending—by balancing them identically with customers' acceptances and letters of credit. This also can-

not be done, and need not be done, with empty balances in accounts.

25 Detailed study of the principles of Objective Economics reveals that at a ratio of about .50, an extremely interesting and complex mathematical singularity occurs. For the record, its two most evident properties are that the "constant of ability to resist change (real entity)" equals the same constant for the imaginary counter-entity, and the "constant of debit and credit spread" equals unity. An ancillary condition of great interest is that the ratio of the "constant of debit and credit cohesion (real entity)" to the same constant for the imaginary counter-entity equals the "constant of best resolution (whole dollars)" for the case in which the debt structure ratio equals unity. This latter condition is clearly trying to tell us something about the relationship between the "divisibility of entities" and the "divisibility of money". I suspect that as our understanding grows we shall discover that when the debt structure ratio has fallen to .50, a viable *bank* is in the making comprising the real entity and its imaginary counter-entity. Specifically, Dome Petroleum, which has had a .50 modality for several years, may be peculiarly competent to become, through judicious merger, a bank.

I hold the discovery of the economic relevance of the "imaginary" to be extremely important, opening to us as it does, the "complex variable." Virtually all real economic acts carry with them an imaginary conjunct. For example, a bank really *does* lend by borrowing since it lends by opening deposit accounts. It does not, however, borrow by opening loan accounts in reality.

26 Thus, even though the money orders are not necessarily "legal tender" they are *loaned* by the banks once deposited because "cashing them in" involves the banks' accepting from the government, money that is a *promise to pay*, i.e. a loan from the banks.

27 These terms were obtained from the Canadian Imperial Bank of Commerce which happens to be my bank and to which I owe a great deal in several ways. I telephoned one of their senior accountants and asked:

"I see you have *identical* entries on both sides of your balance sheet, both called customers' acceptances and letters of credit. What on earth are they?"

"Well", he replied, "customers' acceptances and letters of credit are not *hard* transactions."

"So they are soft?"

"Yes."

28 The specific evidence that soft transactions do annihilate obligations is that they are represented by *identical* entries in both the asset and liabilities sides of the bank's balance sheet. As we shall see later, this annihilation happens extremely quickly in most cases, sometimes, in Bank of Canada dealings, within hours.

29 It is shown in Appendix III that the five leading banks in Canada had a ratio of soft transactions to their total payables that began at 2.96% in 1969, had risen to 5.34% in 1975, dropped to 4.58% in 1977 and had risen to 5.87% in 1979. Preliminary statements suggest it rose again in 1980.

30 Readers who say immediately that it is "obvious" that our dollar must fall

because its "supply" abroad has increased with no apparent increase in its "demand", should reread the last chapter. "Demand and supply economics" are *not* Objective Economics, and we simply cannot disappear into them without walking right back into a subjective economics the relevance of which is denied by the law of constrained fall to states of least economic energy.

Unfortunately I cannot deal adequately with the determination of foreign exchange rates briefly enough to include in this book the theory confirmed by the TSE300 study. This is particularly the case because those rates cannot be treated independently of bank prime rates and bank net worths in all countries and currencies. In general, it will suffice to accept that continued sale of a currency lowers its price in other currencies unless bank loans are very large in volume perhaps as defences against take-overs.

[31] The Bank of Nova Scotia is the one of the "big five" in Canada that appears to have annihilated obligations in this manner extremely aggressively during the gold boom of 1979. Historically except for 1969 and 1970, its ratio of soft transactions to hard has been above average. In 1979, however, that ratio dropped sharply below the five-bank average.

[32] Canadian banks all have had debt structure ratios of 1.02—1.05 for the past 11 years.

[33] That is, until President Nixon stopped selling and buying gold at a fixed price in United States currency.

[34] The fate of net worth in this respect is shown in Appendix III for Canada's big five.

[35] See *How* ALL *Economies Work,* pp. 54, 55.

[36] Just how close Canada's big five come to this is shown in Appendix III.

[37] Bank leverage is $RP = E_t (R+P)/W$. Part of the banking modality is that its debt structure ratio remains near unity. That implies that for each dollar of $R+P$, $R = .50$, and $P = .50$. RP is therefore $.50 \times .50 = .25$. A customer with a debt structure ratio of .50 is breaking below the conservation range for leverage sufficiently that that customer's payables, part of which are bank receivables, must be slightly "expanded" so that RP remains at .25 for the bank. The rate of interest increase is the form that expansion takes. Rather than being an increase in a "price", its nature is more like what is called the "Fitzgerald Contraction" in modern physics, what is being contracted being the capital values of loans as their interest rate rises.

An important discovery of Objective Economics is that at $\alpha = .50$, the increased waiting for which the banks require higher interest rates is also the trigger that can cause the borrower to form a bank with its own imaginary counter-entity. See note 25, and my paper "Dome Canada Limited— Canada's Newest Bank" in Progress Report, February 1981, by the Institute of Objective Economics.

[38] Investment retards the generation of savings that results from deposits passing into loans *and* loans passing into deposits. There is, however, a lag as deposit rates flow into prime lending rates and those primes flow into deposit rates because of maturity dates of the debts involved. Intermediation minimizes this lag.

[39] Both our business media and our technical journals are full of notions of how increased domestic interest rates "attract" foreign investors who buy our dollars to invest and in so doing, raise their price. In contrast, the crucial relation is *the natural reserve ratio of banks* and the three components of the reserve, one of which (generated savings from hard transactions) is pivotal. Decreased interest rates almost *instantly* cause an increase in soft transactions. No "investment decision" is involved. If Canadian bank deposits in United States banks do not annihilate enough (because customers' acceptances from importers from the United States are not sufficient), then the deposits are "sold" into Japanese banks and so on, until the acceptances are found. It is this world-wide search for annihilation of obligations that literally created the Euro-currency market starting in about 1960. The fact is, the world-wide search for customer acceptances with which to annihilate obligations by no means necessarily works out without a residual of deposit liabilities that have not been annihilated. Such residuals were the basis of the Euro-currencies which, instead of being converted and used for local credit creation (hard transactions), are loaned internationally as Euro-currencies usually as US dollars. In actual fact banks sometimes "end up *borrowing*" their own deposits back in Euro-currencies. It would take us too far afield to explain how and why this happens. In his Chapter 13, Blackman (The Canadian Financial System, McGraw-Hill Ryerson, 1980) gives us an excellent introduction to the Euro-currencies.

[40] It is useful to recall that the forced resignation of the second Governor of the Bank of Canada, Mr. James Coyne, happened at precisely the time at which these resistances were gaining high profile in Canada. The Prime Minister, Mr. Diefenbaker, looked at what were then regarded as high interest rates and saw political problems in them. Mr. Coyne looked at a remarkable tendency for sell-off of Canadian dollars if the interest rate did not remain high. He wanted governmental retrenchment. Diefenbaker wanted to win an election. He won and Coyne went.

[41] Warren J. Blackman, op. cit. Chapter 5, especially pp. 100-102.

[42] This is not to say that some government agency (usually the central bank), before deficit financing took the governmental debt structure ratio down to .50, could not (and did not) affect the economy. By bidding up government bills with printed money, it could (and did) flood bank deposits and hence trigger off the mechanisms I have described that relate to the natural reserve ratio of banks. By selling such bills rather than buying them, it can (and does) reverse such easy money "policies". By lowering or raising the reserves expropriated from banks it could (and did) pursue similar "policies", and, in so far as its rediscount rate was used by banks to obtain deposits, it could (and did) use that rate for such policy pursuit. None of these activities, however, makes such an agency a *bank*, and all of them over a succession of government budgets simply reflect the fiscal policies of government which have involved a succession of deficits.

[43] We recall that the banking modality of unit debt structure ratios is one part of the law of constrained fall to states of least economic energy. By increasing interest rates as they interact with increased soft to hard transaction ratios, the banks *could* accommodate a fall of the government's debt struc-

ture ratio below .50. The rise of interest rates as they interact with increased soft to hard transaction ratios measures the economic work the banks would have to do to resist the law of constrained fall and accommodate government. If private banks are to retain their near-maximum leverage as the government is thus accommodated, that economic work must come from outside the private banks since, as is shown in Appendix III, and discussed above, the banks' net worth share of their natural reserves falls as the soft to hard transaction ratio rises. In other words, in the limit, the private banks would "burn out" if an outside source of that work were not available. Central banks are the suppliers of this new and external (to the private banks) economic work. Following an earlier thought, I conceive a central bank-private bank system as a "hybrid" that uses the "fusion" involved in the central bank modality to feed the "fission" involved in the private bank modality.

[44] Theft is not a commonly used alternative for individuals. Most institutions in society, by applying the law, quickly punish many of those who do use it. It is a common alternative for governments historically, largely, I think, because they "make the laws" that define theft. In the eyes of many western Canadians, for example, the Federal Government is currently embarked upon "energy policies" which when put into law will involve legalizing theft.

[45] In the business entity, the distinction between fiscal and monetary policy is represented by the distinction between "running the business", i.e. the whole business, and "collecting receivables and postponing payables". In solvent enterprises, these latter functions are more or less a routine headed up by a comptroller who may or may not be a member of senior management.

[46] As is the case with most short term "commercial paper", T-Bills carry no interest rate on their face. The interest paid is determined by the discount off their face value at which they are sold.

[47] The mechanism of annihilation of obligations most frequently used in the United States is the "rediscount rate" of the Federal Reserve Board, the rate at which it discounts bills from its member banks. The fact the Bank of Canada currently "sets" its rediscount rate at ¼ of 1% above that indicated by the last sale of T-Bills, i.e. the Purchase and Resale rate, simply recognizes that the rediscounting that goes on in Canada is with money market dealers rather than banks.

[48] I first used the pictorial methods that follow in preparing a report under contract for the Federal Government of Canada entitled *Privatization is the Way Out*. The methods were suggested by the full cost revenue dependency concept being recommended for the Federal Government in the book *The Way Out* by A.R. Bailey/D.G. Hull, The Institute for Research on Public Policy, 1980.

[49] I ask the technical reader not to expect, nor to look for, rigor in these illustrations. In fact to use them I have dropped back from the objective methods underlying the new science to the subjective concept of "importance". The derivation of the precise loci of our debt structure ratio arcs and of the orthogonal properties of AB and CB require a level of abstraction

that will be found in *How* ALL *Economies Work*, Ch's VIII and IX.

[50] A technical reader will realize that for my first grid square the axes are pay*ment* in the two senses of receipt and payment of payables. For grid squares outside that one, however, the two axes are pay*ables* in the senses of receivables and payables. We all know, however, that pay*ables* become pay*ments*. That fact encourages us to try to formulate the problem of *resolving* our geometry so that our axes have uniformity of meaning, however abstract. Discovering how to do this is the essence of Objective Economics and of dimensionless science in general.

[51] See Chapter 2, p. 18.

[52] The actual calculations from what are called the Einstein and Minkowski Conditions to 5 decimal points are as follows:

	EINSTEIN	MINKOWSKI
α	Importance of collecting (not paying) a dollar	Importance of generating a receivable dollar (not generating a payable dollar)
.50	1.56964	1.87728
.40	1.70835	1.90000
.30	1.90196	1.92364
.29	1.92527	1.92605
	—scientific bankruptcy—	
.28	1.94940	1.92848
.27	1.97438	1.93091
.20	2.17501	1.94819

The left hand column of calculated lengths refers to the lengths of successions of *pairs* of arc lengths. The right hand column refers to intersections of *pairs* of straight line lengths.

[53] On the surface it might appear that privatization, i.e. the sale of government assets, is an alternative to cutting expenditures as the Reagan administration is committed to do. This is true as long as the government's debt structure ratio has not fallen into the bankruptcy range below .289. If it has then the only alternative is: "does the government sell its assets or mine?" The essential point is that if a government is in the bankruptcy range, it cannot both "hold the line" on interest costs and maintain its currency value. It must face either sharply rising interest costs or sharply falling currency values. Sometimes it will likely face both. If the United States Government is in the bankruptcy range, as I believe it is, therefore, either rising interest cost or a falling United States dollar will destroy the Reagan effort to cut expenditures. The cut in tax rates, however, will likely be achieved but it will not yield more tax revenue as Dr. Laffer claims. It will yield less because of higher interest costs and/or lower currency values.

[54] These additional intersections in the Einstein Conditions underlying Objective Economics are called the Lee-Whiting Conditions after their discoverer, Dr. Lee-Whiting, a mathematical physicist at Atomic Energy of Canada Limited. That discovery was part of his response to my *Hanna Lec-*

tures in Dimensionless Physics, presented to a group of AECL physicists in November, 1978. The interpretation of the conditions is entirely my responsibility.

[55] Banks of course have buildings and processing equipment of various types on all of which they accumulate depreciation. The amount accumulated annually, however, is rarely more than 1% of total assets of the bank. Accumulated depreciation of a car manufacturer, and indeed of most established manufacturers, is a much larger proportion of assets.

[56] Full details of this study were published by the Wall Street Transcript, December 22, 1980, pp. 60,060-65.

[57] The generated savings resulting from the annihilation mechanism is growing rapidly for Canada's banks and doing so at the expense of the net worth share of their value. This can be seen in Appendix III. The major growth, however, has been in the last two or three years which means that omitting this item in the valuation study did not introduce significant error when all 300 companies were aggregated.

[58] It might appear that on this definition of natural value by issuing large enough amounts of the currency we can always restore the natural value of a dollar to almost a dollar. In fact, however, such issue increases the natural value of banks very rapidly which increases inflation pari passu.

[59] Bank executives tend not to emphasize the entropy-like increase in trading. They emphasize the insufficiency of net worth "cover" which implies that, given a default by a major customer, they are in danger of defaulting themselves.

[60] My examination of both Massey's and Chrysler's books indicates that neither has been even close to scientific bankruptcy ($\alpha = .289$). Both, however, have had sharp decrcases in their debt structure ratios that posed the banks problems to which they could not respond. Both are cases of what I call "hot money" or "second order" insolvency.

[61] Perhaps the most foolish statement about the economy ever made by a political leader has been made and often repeated by Pierre Trudeau the present Prime Minister of Canada. In "justifying" a succession of encroachments on the economy by his insolvent government he alleges that the "free market system" does not work as well as it should. The White Knight of government therefore is needed. The reason the free market system works badly is the tremendous locking up of economic energies we can never retrieve, in trading, that is forced upon the system by the very insolvency of his government. That insolvency has chased Canadian banks into soft transactions at the expense of their net worth as a fox scatters chickens.

[62] Marx's venom, petty as it often was, has puzzled scholars for years. In part it may have sprung from his lifetime travail with boils, surely one of the most painful annoyances of life. Some years ago I spent an evening in Zaltbommel, Holland, with an elderly lady who said her family had a letter written by Karl when 12 years old to his aunt in Zaltbommel (a Philips, an ancestor of the Philips of Philips Electric which family founded a bank in Zaltbommel). She said the letter thanks his aunt for his prior visit to her

and tells her that he had been to the doctor for "boils in the crotch". My God! For a man who spent most of his time from 1849 to 1883, when he died, *sitting* in the British Museum reading government reports, such an affliction would be unbearable. Interestingly enough, Lenin also had a severe debility in the form of searing headaches and Stalin had a deformity in one of his arms. He may also have had chronic hangovers judging from his alleged appetite for vodka.

63 Though commenting on it is beyond the scope of this book, I refer readers to the important book by the Russian mathematician, Igor Shafarevich, *The Socialist Phenomenon*, Harper & Row, 1980, English edition. His tracing of much of socialism to the Anabaptist tradition (which summary vastly understates his thesis) goes a long way to explaining the profound tendency for all Communist regimes to contain an elect that is almost callously indifferent to the masses it governs.

64 In *Capitalism and the Historians* (University of Chicago Press, 1954), F.A. Hayek and other writers examined contemporary reports of conditions in England. As Hayek wrote: "...most of the assertions to which (a socialist interpretation of history) has given the status of 'facts which everybody knows' have long been proved not to have been facts at all..."

65 As evidence of how even the greatest of minds can be swayed by near trivia, Hegel saw his dialectic process as leading to the hegemony of the German State. Another Hegelian scholar, the German Catholic Schlegel, used Hegel's dialectic to argue that the end of the historical process was the hegemony of the Roman Catholic Church. Alfred Marshall, who in many respects shared fatherhood of the current subjective economics with Mill (although I suspect he would deny he ever knew its mother in many cases), is also credited with a "wants-activities" dialectic by the American sociologist, Talcott Parsons. Marshall's dialectic appears to have said that "the Manchester merchant shall inherit the earth". In my book, *How ALL Economies Work*, (pp 5-6), I referred to Georgescu-Roegen's identification of the subjective economics as itself being a dialectic. Thus Marx is not unique in imposing the teleology of a dialectic on the economic process.

66 He did, however, have an intensely practical background in organizing unions of the Baku oil field workers, a background most of his contemporaries of the first decade of this century, including the émigré Lenin, did not have. Stalin has to be conceded to have been an expert not only in this role that was consistent with classical Marxism, i.e. the struggle of labor against capital, but he also had much experience with ethnic minorities who brought ideological conflicts to Marx's doctrine that were frequently resolved by bullets. Marx himself had little patience with ethnic minorities. Lenin's interest in them after 1917 was a matter of practical politics that he left largely to Stalin.

67 See Deutscher op. cit., p. 576.

68 David Ricardo was an English stockbroker who piled up a fortune early in life, bought an estate and "retired" to it to do chemical experiments, ponder about economics, and be an activist in politics. Publication of his economic thought was pressed on him by friends, one of whom was James Mill, the father of J.S. Mill. Ricardo had an analytical genius that I think

was relatively lacking in Smith. His thought had much to do with creating the tendency of English-speaking economists to emphasize the supply side of the demand and supply "equation". The most famous doctrine attributed to him and the one Marx virtually took over without even noting Ricardo's concern about it was the *Iron Law of Wages*. The Marxian interpretation of this law is that, in a capitalist economy, wages always tend to the subsistence level of laborers. To Ricardo, this law was at best a first approximation.

[69] See Mao Tse-tung: "On the Correct Handling of Contradictions among the People" (February, 1957). Translated in *Essential Works of Chinese Communism* edited by Winberg Chai, Bantam Books, 1969, pp 305—312.

[70] In effect, therefore, Objective Economics leads us to a theory of natural law about why banks are formed. Instead of a Medici waking up one morning and saying "I am going to start a bank", the day comes when he says, "By God! I have a bank." Conversely, if we have such a theory of natural law we also have a theory of the same nature that tells us the circumstances in which the production of "goods" rather than money is necessary. Goods production does not follow from human needs in any relevant sense. It follows from the less than maximum leverage of entities that have tended to debt structure ratios of .82 (least investment) and .70 (least generated savings).

[71] The ownership structure ratio was first introduced in lectures given to a group of Toronto professionals in the spring of 1981. It is not contained in *How ALL Economies Work* and in fact could not be discovered until the TSE 300 study was analyzed.

[72] It is interesting that many balance sheets are so labelled that net worth, or the "capital account", is taken as part of liabilities. Indeed in most cases the whole side of the balance sheet that balances assets is called "liabilities".

[73] In this discovery, which I emphasize is empirical and can be confirmed by anyone willing to consult enough balance sheets, the economic relevance of one of the institutions about which Marxists make so much noise, falls to the ground. This is the institution of the legal system which Marxists allege simply mirrors capitalism. *The natural laws of the economy act as if the legal system did not exist*, for the distinction between debt and equity, a distinction those natural laws refuse to make, is part of jurisprudence. One of the reasons the subjective economics even in the hands of a master such as Böhm-Bawerk was only able to convert the converted in attacking Marxism is that statutory law is fundamental to the subjectivist and yet he has no comments to make about it. It just "is" and the economy as he visualizes it works within its framework, a framework that distinguishes ownership from debt. There is no evidence of the relevance of such a distinction in natural objective economics.

[74] From time to time Marx and Lenin both referred to the exploitation of women, seeing them essentially as prostitutes within the marriages of capitalist societies. Shafarevich traces this view through the Anabaptist tradition. The long-sufferings of the wives of Marx and Lenin (who publicly thrust a mistress on his wife into the bargain) and the suicide of Stalin's first wife are well-known and suggest that the exploitation concept was

gained at first hand.

75 That other great whipping stake of inflation, namely, energy prices, has also not been mentioned. Energy prices are financed by inflation and in that sense are its result rather than its cause. There is more to be said, however, about energy prices. Deficit financing has caused falling debt structure ratios and hence the "inefficiency" of inflation (i.e. much more than least generated savings and investment and much less than maximum leverage). Similarly, however, the OPEC governments, and those of Alberta and Mexico more recently, have created very high debt structure ratios for themselves. That also causes the inefficiency of inflation because of sharp departures from least generated savings and investment and maximum leverage. Coming on the heels of the early days of Euro-currencies which themselves represented an overall tendency for countries' private banks to dump currency in response to mounting low debt structure ratio government insolvency, the most profound effect of the OPEC adventure has been to multiply the Euro-currency pool many times over. This has the effect of poisoning the annihilation mechanism of all banks and has led to much recycling by private banks of what are essentially their own deposits. Even though Euro-currency rates of interest appear to be low, no rate is low if the banks borrowing from the Euro-currency market in actual fact are *adding* that rate to their original deposit rate. In other words, the most baleful effects of OPEC now are giving what are already very high rates of interest a sharp upward bias and steadily adding to the non-annihilated obligations of the private banking system. Carried to the ultimate, the OPEC adventure will "quench" the private banking system as it drowns in its own non-annihilated obligations.

76 To pursue my metaphor a bit further, years ago a friend of mine was interviewing a female prisoner at Kingston Penitentiary in his capacity as prison psychologist. When he commented on her occupation as a prostitute to feed her heroin habit she said:

"Do you have any ideas about how else I can earn $100 a day?"

He had none. Many members of the money market are caught in just such bewilderment.

77 A few years ago the Parliament of Canada received a rude shock to its national pride when the Bank of Canada had to register a large debt offering in the United States with the Securities Exchange Commission. There is simply no justification for governments, particularly central governments, being exempted from such normal and proper procedures either domestically or internationally. The only credit worthiness that ever need concern the lender is the one he is unable to examine.

To offer an example almost concomitant with publication of this book, buyers of government T-bills in the past 3 months have had no idea that Prime Minister Trudeau would blow several million dollars on highly questionable trips to Africa and the Philippines and that while in Africa he would give $10 million to the International Research and Development Agency.

78 The second ratio that I call the "ownership structure ratio" that is defined by net worth plus generated savings divided by the value the stock market

gives to the entity was used in Chapter 17. That ratio is also limited by the law of constrained fall in precisely the same manner as is the debt structure ratio. As a result of this discovery, we know that neither the debt nor equity portions of the proposed package can increase without limit without the creation of some insolvencies. The fundamental hope of mankind is that the size of the package required to do its two jobs is not so great that we must replace the present inflation that is caused by governmental insolvency with one that is caused by private insolvency. If that hope fails then "funds" are simply growing faster than the world economy can accommodate without inflation. Thus by preparing too extensively for our future (as with pension funds) we create the necessity of our pensions being depreciated when we receive them.

[79] I am grateful to Prof. David Cape for emphasizing that least generated savings is the "most efficient use of money" and to Mr. Ross Healy, President of the Toronto Society of Financial Analysts, for emphasizing that least investment is the "most efficient use of goods".

[80] My studies reveal that neither Massey nor Chrysler has really fallen into insolvency. Both, however, have had sharp decreases in their debt structure ratios. I refer to their problems as "second order" or "hot money" insolvency. Were central banks not monopolizing the money market, both cases probably could have been handled without difficulty.

[81] The Bank of England was formed in the late 17th century because the government had defaulted on its debt to London's goldsmiths, the "bankers" of the day. The fundamental problem of government, therefore, was how, short of a reign of terror, it could again be accepted into the economy as a borrower and lender. The Bank of England was the solution. To my knowledge it cost no heads but its existence did continue to bankrupt bankers for at least 30 years.

APPENDIX I

Discovered Central Tendencies Justifying the Law of Constrained Fall to States of Least Economic Energy

In this Appendix, starting with Bell Canada's 1979 balance sheet, how the debt structure ratio was calculated is shown, i.e. what goes into total receivables and total payables is made explicit. Frequency distributions are then shown for debt structure ratio occurrences for all companies for seven years along with sums of net worth, sums of stock market value, and sums of generated savings for ranges of the debt structure ratio. Finally, each of these four quantities is shown by individual year 1973—1979 for debt structure ratios ranging from .49—.58 up to 1.39—1.48.

Consolidated Balance Sheet

As at December 31

Bell Canada 1979

		Thousands of dollars	
Assets		**1979**	**1978**
Telecommunications property – at cost (note 8)	Buildings, plant and equipment	$9,741,337	$8,826,260
	Less: Accumulated depreciation	2,950,562	2,614,419
		6,790,775	6,211,841
	Land	65,153	61,833
	Plant under construction	270,089	221,181
	Material and supplies	128,971	107,746
		7,254,988	6,602,601
Manufacturing property – at cost (note 8)	Buildings, plant and equipment	680,274	590,243
	Less: Accumulated depreciation	274,868	234,651
		405,406	355,592
	Land	13,353	12,796
		418,759	368,388
		7,673,747	6,970,989
Investments	Associated companies and non-consolidated subsidiaries – at equity (note 1)	417,403	151,318
	Other	4,832	5,723
		422,235	157,041
Current assets	Cash and temporary cash investments – at cost (approximates market)	95,286	228,986
	Accounts receivable – principally from customers (including $5,903 (1978 – $3,598) from associated companies)	1,060,145	773,496
	Inventories (note 9)	492,539	361,402
	Other (principally prepaid expenses)	106,519	77,877
		1,754,489	1,441,761
Other assets	Cash and temporary cash investments held for contract operations – at cost (approximates market)	49,532	91,851
	Long term receivables	41,296	44,932
	Deferred charges		
	contract operations	90,583	112,912
	unrealized foreign currency losses, less amortization	131,780	165,162
	other	82,663	84,371
	Cost of shares in acquired subsidiaries in excess of underlying net assets, less amortization (note 1)	119,163	127,989
	Other	11,025	8,275
		526,042	635,492
	Total assets	**$10,376,513**	**$9,205,283**

On behalf of the Board of Directors:

H. Clifford Hatch
Director

Marcel Bélanger
Director

		Thousands of dollars	
Liabilities and Shareholders' Equity		1979	1978
Capital stock authorized (note 10)			
Common shareholders' equity	Common shares outstanding (note 11)	$1,320,647	$1,176,622
	Premium on capital stock	807,778	607,388
	Contributed surplus	15,290	15,290
	Retained earnings	1,198,384	1,041,075
		3,342,099	2,840,375
Convertible preferred shares (redeemable) (note 12)		216,718	290,765
Non-convertible preferred shares (redeemable) (note 12)		112,255	113,965
Minority interest in subsidiary	Preferred shares	30,324	30,908
companies	Common shares	437,417	265,770
		467,741	296,678
Long term debt (including unrealized foreign currency losses) (note 13)		3,675,103	3,381,086
Current liabilities	Accounts payable	570,956	477,831
	Advance billing for service	52,445	49,617
	Dividends payable	72,540	60,889
	Taxes accrued	73,433	110,879
	Interest accrued	78,875	71,497
	Debt due within one year (note 14)	306,086	280,796
		1,154,335	1,051,509
Deferred credits	Income taxes	1,066,749	933,900
	Other (note 15)	341,513	297,005
		1,408,262	1,230,905
Commitments and contingent liabilities (notes 8 and 15)			
	Total liabilities and shareholders' equity	**$10,376,513**	**$9,205,283**

G. L. Henthorn
Vice-President & Comptroller

Calculation of the Debt Structure Ratio (α)

BELL CANADA December 31, 1979

Receivables   thousands of dollars

Cash and temporary cash investments .... $ 95,286
Accounts receivable   1,060,145
Prepaid expenses   106,519
Associated companies   417,403
Other investments   4,832
Cash, etc. from contract operations   49,532
Accumulated depreciation (total)   3,225,430
Long term receivables   41,296

    RECEIVABLES $ 5,000,443

Payables

Total Liabilities and Shareholders Equity (TLSE) $10,376,513
Preferred Stock (total) .... $ (328,973)
Common shares outstanding .... (1,320,647)
Premium on capital stock ....   (807,778)
Retained earnings .... (1,198,384)
Contributed surplus ....   (15,290)
Net Worth (N) $(3,671,072)   (3,671,072)

    PAYABLES = TLSE − N $ 6,705,441

Debt Structure Ratio = (Receivables)/(Payables) = α = .75

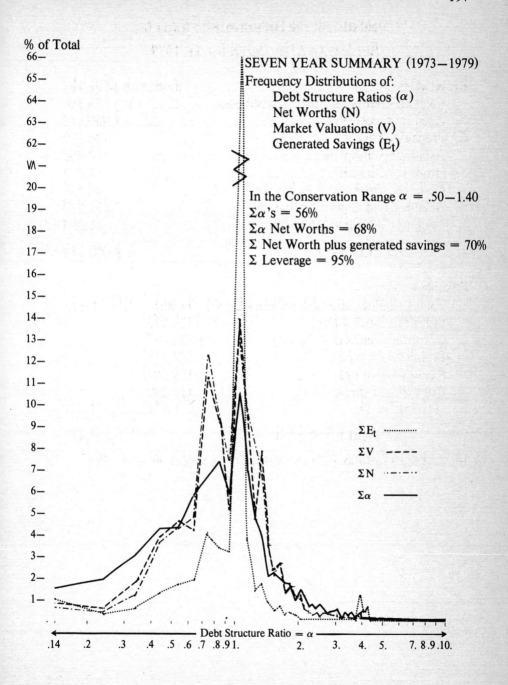

% of Total

SEVEN YEAR SUMMARY (1973—1979)
Frequency Distributions of:
    Debt Structure Ratios (α)
    Net Worths (N)
    Market Valuations (V)
    Generated Savings (E_t)

In the Conservation Range $\alpha = .50-1.40$
$\Sigma\alpha$'s $= 56\%$
$\Sigma\alpha$ Net Worths $= 68\%$
Σ Net Worth plus generated savings $= 70\%$
Σ Leverage $= 95\%$

ΣE_t ....
ΣV - - - -
ΣN -·-·-·-
$\Sigma\alpha$ ————

Debt Structure Ratio $= \alpha$

.14   .2   .3   .4 .5 .6 .7 .8 .9 1.   2.   3.   4.   5.   7. 8 .9 .10.

198

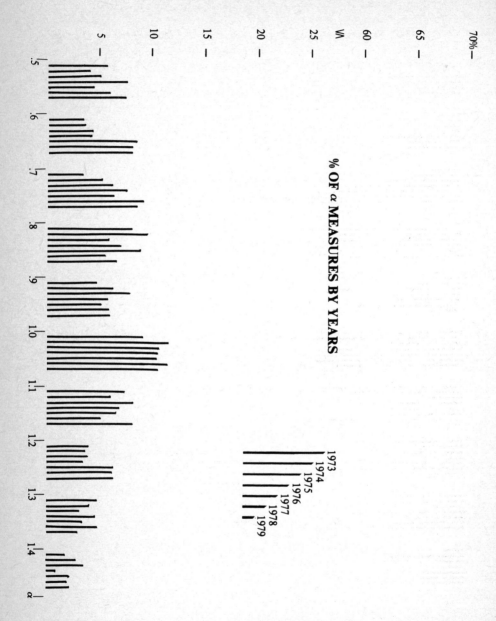

% OF α MEASURES BY YEARS

199

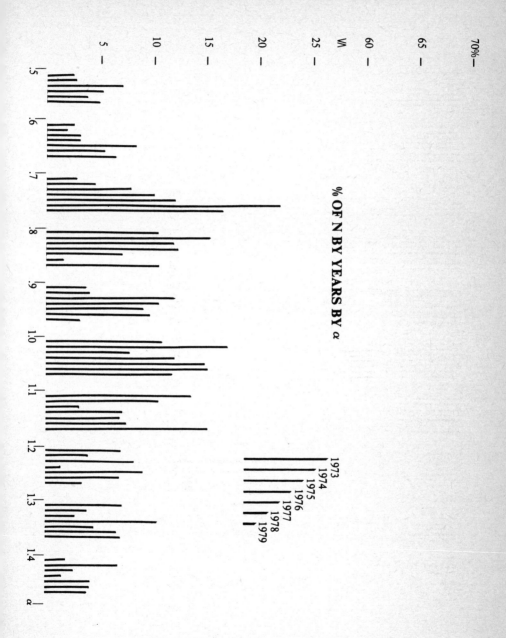

% OF N BY YEARS BY α

1973
1974
1975
1976
1977
1978
1979

200

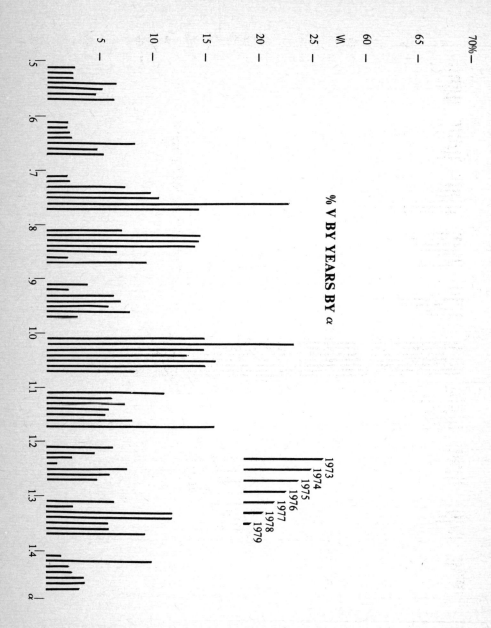

% V BY YEARS BY α

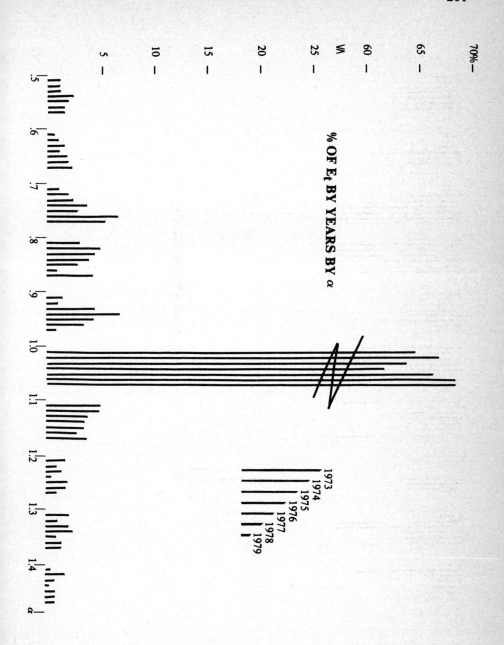

% OF E_t BY YEARS BY α

APPENDIX II

Calculation of Generated Savings (E_t), Investment (W), and Leverage (L)

Bell Canada (1979) $ 000
   Total Receivables (R) $ 5,000,443
   Total Payables (P)   6,705,441
   R/P (debt structure ratio) $= \alpha = .75$

Referring to *Tables of Atrill's Constants* by Prof. J.M. McNamee for $\alpha = .75$ the values of four dimensionless numbers symbolized by c, m, c^1, m^1, are found to be

$c = 3.16$

$m = 19.29$

$c^1 = 1.47$

$m^1 = 32.59$

The formula for E_t in $000's is

$$E_t = \frac{R + P}{m(c)^2} + \frac{R + P}{m^1(c^1)^2}$$

Substituting the actual values we obtain

$$E_t = \frac{11,705,884}{192.62} + \frac{11,705,884}{70.42} = 60,771 + 166,299 = 227,001$$

Note that this $227,001,000 of generated savings is approximately 2% of the sum R + P. This is broadly true for all companies with α's between .50 and 2.00.

Investment W is defined as $E_t/R + E_t/P = E_t(R+P)/RP$

For BTC in 1979, therefore, it was .0792. It depends only upon the debt structure ratio and not the absolute values of R and P.

Leverage L is defined as $RP = E_t(R+P)/W$. It is $3,353 \times 10^{19}$.

Per dollar of (R+P), E_t, W, and L are all marked on the graph that follows.

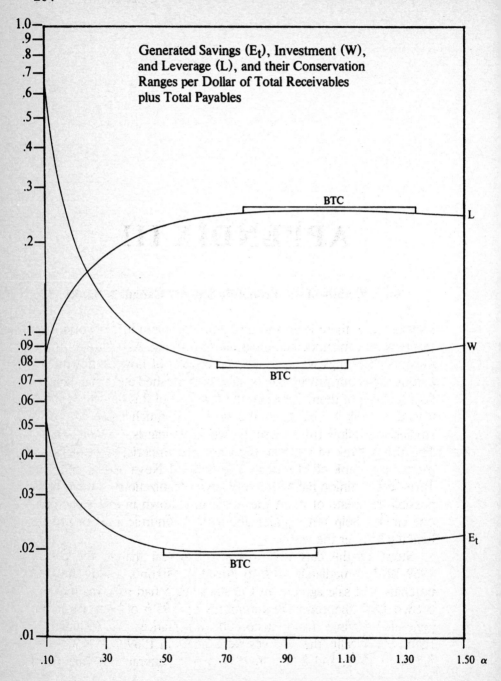

Generated Savings (E_t), Investment (W), and Leverage (L), and their Conservation Ranges per Dollar of Total Receivables plus Total Payables

APPENDIX III

Some Details of the Economic State of Canada's Banks

I suggest that there is no more urgent a problem in the world than rectifying our misunderstandings about banking. As a result of those misunderstandings we have little perception of how far down dangerous roads our private banks have been pushed and what dangers lie just ahead of them. I present the few facts of this Appendix about Canada's "Big 5" banks in the hope that much more extensive studies will follow from them. By world standards, Canada's Big 5, The Royal Bank of Canada, the Canadian Imperial Bank of Commerce, the Bank of Montreal, The Bank of Nova Scotia, and The Toronto-Dominion Bank, are very large organizations. If it has been possible to create of them the wasteland shown in this Appendix, one cannot help but wonder about the economic state of private banking all over the world.

Study of the data that follow will reveal that in the period 1969-1972 immediately prior to President Nixon's cutting the gold purchase and sale agreement Canada's Big 5 had reserves that exceeded their theoretical requirements of 7.95% of payables if the generated savings from customers' acceptances are included in them. Specifically, the reserves were 8.53% in 1969, 8.55% in 1970, 8.53% in 1971, and 8.45% in 1972. If the generated savings from customers' acceptances are excluded, these reserves become respectively, 7.86%, 7.77%, 7.73% and 7.65%.

In 1969, 47.6% of the reserves of the Big 5 were in the form of generated savings from hard transactions and 44.6% were in the form of net worth. Only 7.8% were in the form of generated savings from soft transactions. In 1980, however, only 44.9% were in the form of generated savings from hard transactions, 31.2% were in the form of net worth, and fully 23.9% were in the form of generated savings from soft transactions. Further, whereas the reserves including those generated by soft transactions were at their 12-year high of 8.91%, excluding those in that category, reserves dropped to the 12-year low of 6.78%.

The very least these data imply is that as our Big 5 are pushed more and more out of the credit-creating business by central banking activity and more and more into the business of simply moving credit around, the pressure on them to raise rates on existing call loans mounts steadily. On the other hand, their purchase of foreign currency, chiefly US currency, is pressed ever upwards as the same pressure lowers the price of the dollar.

The sharp drop in the net worth share of reserves (from 44.6% to 31.2% in 12 years) is a new way of stating what banks already know: namely, their net worth "cover" has long since passed beneath acceptable minima. This leaves them using the raising of rates on existing call loans in their competitive struggles with other banks in cases in which, a decade ago, bank net worths would have been used for cover and credit would have been expanded.

Natural Reserves* of the Big 5 Banks in Canada

(1969) — 1980)

Year	Generated Savings Hard-Transactions- 10^6	Total	Soft 10^6	Total	Net Worth 10^6	% of Total	Total Natural Reserves	% of Bank Payables
1969	1473.1	47.6	241.2	7.8	1381.4	44.6	3095.7	8.53(7.86)**
Cumulative	1473.1	47.6	241.2	7.8	1381.4	44.6	3095.7	8.53
1970	1624.7	47.4	313.1	9.1	1487.3	43.4	3425.1	8.55(7.77)
Cumulative	3097.8	47.5	554.3	8.5	2868.7	44.0	6520.8	8.54
1971	1824.8	47.6	359.2	9.4	1647.1	43.0	3831.1	8.53(7.73)
Cumulative	4922.6	47.5	913.5	8.8	4514.8	43.6	10351.9	8.54
1972	2103.0	48.1	414.9	9.5	1857.4	42.4	4374.8	8.45(7.65)
Cumulative	7025.6	47.7	1328.4	9.0	6372.2	43.3	14726.7	8.51
1973	2610.1	50.9	523.8	10.2	1995.9	38.9	5129.7	7.98(7.16)
Cumulative	9635.7	48.5	1852.2	9.3	8368.1	42.1	19856.4	8.37
1974	3135.8	50.6	885.3	14.3	2177.7	35.1	6198.8	8.00(6.86)
Cumulative	12771.5	49.0	2737.5	10.5	10545.8	40.5	26055.2	8.28
1975	3566.7	48.8	1052.2	14.4	2683.9	36.7	7302.9	8.31(7.11)
Cumulative	16338.2	48.9	3789.7	11.4	13229.7	39.6	33358.1	8.28
1976	4138.4	50.4	1058.9	12.9	3008.2	36.7	8205.5	8.03(6.99)
Cumulative	20476.6	49.3	4848.6	11.7	16237.9	39.0	41563.6	8.23
1977	5011.0	51.5	1271.1	13.0	3453.2	35.5	9735.3	7.83(6.81)
Cumulative	25487.6	49.7	6119.7	11.9	19691.1	38.4	51298.9	8.15
1978	6128.4	51.0	1640.6	13.6	4259.1	35.4	12028.0	7.96(6.87)
Cumulative	31616.0	49.9	7760.3	12.2	23950.2	37.8	63326.9	8.12
1979	7413.0	49.9	2407.3	16.2	5043.1	33.9	14863.4	8.11(6.79)
Cumulative	39029.0	49.9	10167.6	13.0	28993.3	37.1	78190.3	8.11
1980	8705.5	44.9	4629.9	23.9	6043.6	31.2	19382.0	8.91(6.78)
Cumulative	47737.5	48.9	14797.5	15.2	35036.9	35.9	97572.3	8.26

*NaturalReserves of Banks are their generated savings from hard and soft transactions plus their net worth.
** The values in parentheses omit generated savings from soft transactions.

Statistical Summary of Recent Big 5 History

Generated Savings	shown as E_t
Net Worth	shown as N
Customers' Acceptances	shown as C
Generated Savings from C	shown as (E_t)
Natural Reserves	shown as $[N + E_t + (E_t)]$
Total Payables	shown as P
Natural Reserve Ratio %	shown as $[N + E_t + (E_t)]/P$ (RR%)

	Royal	CIBC	BM	BNS	T-D	Big 5
				($ millions)		
1969						
E_t	386.3	349.9	310.2	228.2	198.5	1473.1
N	375.0	372.1	291.6	168.5	174.2	1381.4
C	310.5	231.1	220.0	152.8	162.6	1077.0
(E_t)	69.5	51.8	49.3	34.2	36.4	241.2
$[N + E_t + (E_t)]$	830.8	773.8	651.1	430.9	409.1	3095.7
P	9510.6	8596.6	7641.3	5622.7	4895.4	36266.6
RR%	8.73	9.00	8.52	7.66	8.36	8.53
1970						
E_t	425.7	420.2	330.3	242.2	206.3	1624.7
N	391.0	402.0	302.9	211.0	180.4	1487.3
C	479.1	303.8	274.6	183.8	156.4	1397.7
(E_t)	107.3	68.1	61.5	41.2	35.0	313.1
$[N + E_t + (E_t)]$	924.0	890.3	694.7	494.4	421.7	3425.1
P	10488.4	10344.7	8152.5	5974.4	5085.8	40045.8
RR%	8.81	8.61	8.52	8.27	8.29	8.55
1971						
E_t	490.5	431.6	390.1	267.8	244.8	1824.8
N	407.8	427.9	315.0	250.2	246.2	1647.1
C	480.4	353.5	250.8	238.1	280.9	1603.7
(E_t)	107.6	79.2	56.2	53.3	62.9	359.2
$[N + E_t + (E_t)]$	1005.9	938.7	761.3	571.3	553.9	3831.1
P	12065.0	10618.9	9599.5	6596.9	6022.0	44902.3
RR%	8.34	8.84	7.93	8.66	9.19	8.53
1972						
E_t	563.7	505.3	430.5	321.5	282.0	2103.0
N	442.3	459.2	364.4	290.3	301.2	1857.4
C	446.1	388.4	373.3	326.3	318.1	1852.2
(E_t)	99.9	87.0	83.6	73.1	71.3	414.9
$[N + E_t + (E_t)]$	1105.9	1051.0	878.5	684.9	654.5	4374.8
P	13879.0	12453.0	10585.6	7925.2	6928.4	51771.2
RR%	7.97	8.44	8.30	8.64	9.45	8.45

	Royal	CIBC	BM	BNS	T-D	Big 5
1973						
E_t	698.7	615.9	550.9	389.9	354.7	2610.1
N	491.3	495.7	390.7	320.2	298.0	1995.9
C	642.8	446.7	434.1	413.7	400.9	2338.2
(E_t)	143.9	100.1	97.2	92.7	89.8	523.8
$[N+E_t+(E_t)]$	1333.9	1211.7	1038.8	802.8	742.5	5129.7
P	17229.5	15159.2	13584.6	9593.7	8723.5	64290.5
RR%	7.74	7.99	7.65	8.37	8.51	7.98
1974						
E_t	806.1	721.1	660.5	502.0	446.1	3135.8
N	516.8	520.3	402.8	403.2	334.6	2177.7
C	1248.9	650.0	816.9	704.7	532.6	3953.1
(E_t)	279.7	145.6	182.9	157.8	119.3	885.3
$[N+E_t+(E_t)]$	1602.6	1387.0	1246.2	1063.0	900.0	6198.8
P	19904.1	17776.4	16431.2	12354.6	10989.7	77456.0
RR%	8.05	7.80	7.58	8.60	8.19	8.00
1975						
E_t	950.3	837.7	686.7	590.1	501.9	3566.7
N	743.3	573.1	451.1	475.0	441.4	2683.9
C	1070.8	1018.1	840.3	1009.6	759.0	4697.8
(E_t)	239.8	228.0	188.2	226.2	170.0	1052.2
$[N+E_t+(E_t)]$	1933.5	1638.8	1326.8	1291.3	1113.3	7302.9
P	23397.0	20667.7	16951.2	14521.3	12376.1	87913.3
RR%	8.26	7.93	7.82	8.89	8.99	8.31
1976						
E_t	1093.8	991.5	771.4	677.2	604.5	4138.4
N	730.9	639.5	541.2	606.0	490.6	3008.2
C	1108.1	984.7	927.7	880.9	826.0	4727.4
(E_t)	248.2	220.6	207.8	197.3	185.0	1058.9
$[N+E_t+(E_t)]$	2072.9	1851.6	1520.4	1480.5	1280.1	8205.5
P	26992.6	24479.8	19023.5	16694.0	14875.4	102065.3
RR%	7.68	7.56	7.99	8.87	8.61	8.03
1977						
E_t	1304.8	1204.5	953.4	837.9	710.4	5011.0
N	854.2	711.3	665.8	681.1	540.8	3453.2
C	1289.1	1281.4	996.6	1060.2	1047.5	5674.8
(E_t)	288.7	287.0	223.2	237.4	234.6	1271.1
$[N+E_t+(E_t)]$	2447.7	2202.8	1842.4	1756.4	1485.8	9735.3
P	32207.0	29976.5	23512.9	20617.9	17997.2	124311.5
RR%	7.60	7.35	7.84	8.52	8.26	7.83
1978						
E_t	1539.4	1451.1	1205.8	1046.3	885.8	6128.4
N	1078.9	910.4	867.7	771.4	630.7	4259.1
C	1861.8	1522.4	1497.4	1130.8	1311.6	7324.0
(E_t)	417.0	341.0	335.4	253.3	293.8	1640.6
$[N+E_t+(E_t)]$	3035.3	2702.5	2408.9	2070.9	1810.3	12028.0
P	37963.8	35839.5	29725.1	25784.4	21839.3	151152.1
RR%	7.99	7.54	8.10	8.03	8.29	7.96

	Royal	CIBC	BM	BNS	T-D	Big 5
1979						
E_t	1925.8	1720.8	1403.6	1316.5	1046.3	7413.0
N	1292.5	1039.7	991.6	977.4	741.9	5043.1
C	2907.9	2140.9	2577.3	1451.7	1669.2	10747.0
(E_t)	651.4	479.6	577.3	325.2	373.9	2407.3
$[N + E_t + (E_t)]$	3869.7	3240.0	2972.5	2619.1	2162.1	14863.4
P	47521.5	42813.9	34611.4	32439.8	25798.2	183184.8
RR%	8.14	7.57	8.59	8.07	8.38	8.11
1977						
E_t	2231.7	2001.7	1709.2	1572.2	1193.7	8708.5
N	1685.8	1111.2	1255.2	1098.2	893.2	6043.6
C	5433.2	4343.6	4915.9	2827.7	3149.0	20669.4
(E_t)	1217.0	972.9	1101.2	633.4	705.4	4629.9
$[N + E_t + (E_t)]$	5134.5	4085.8	4065.6	3303.8	2792.3	19382.0
P	55714.7	49973.4	42670.9	39250.8	29799.7	217409.5
RR%	9.21	8.17	9.52	8.42	9.37	8.91

Index